MOUTHFUL
SIMPLE & STUNNING PARTY FOOD
DANIELLE BOWATER

First edition published in 2005 by Awa Press,
PO Box 11-416, Wellington, New Zealand

National Library of New Zealand Cataloguing-in-Publication Data
Bowater, Danielle.
Mouthful : simple & stunning party food / by Danielle Bowater;
with photographs by Shaun Cato-Symonds. 1st ed.
Includes index.
ISBN 0-9582509-4-4
1. Appetizers. 2. Buffets (Cookery)
I. Cato-Symonds, Shaun.
II. Title
641.812—dc 22

This book is set in Clarendon and Frutiger

Printed by Everbest Printing Company, China

www.awapress.com

MOUTHFUL
SIMPLE & STUNNING PARTY FOOD
DANIELLE BOWATER

Photography   **Shaun Cato-Symonds**

Food Styling   **Anne Wendelken**

Book Design   **Eyework**

AWA PRESS

Contents

I have come to realise that my life has been shaped by food. It all started in the womb, when my mother, Lyndi, craved strawberries with onion dip. She also craved tomato sandwiches – which, as my father Ken attests, were similarly hard to come by in the winter of 1978.

As a youngster I was a fussy eater, surviving on onions, custard, mashed potato and Milo, although thankfully not all at once. I wasn't quick to master the necessary skills of eating either, preferring to shove mashed potato in my ears. I have since made up for this slow start.

Our family has a legacy of creative cooks. My beloved great-grandmother, Vera, had many fantastic recipes, from classic preserves to home-made cough remedies. My maternal grandmother, Margaret, was a caterer famous for her desserts, while my paternal grandmother, Shirley, still makes and sells scrumptious toffees and fudges at markets in our home town of Nelson.

But it was my mother who taught me to cook. From an early age I would help her out in the kitchen. Initially this involved climbing into cupboards and getting into the cayenne pepper but I soon progressed to my first solo effort: a dinner of nachos. I still have my mother's handwritten instructions.

After leaving home, I graduated into cooking in a student flat – a challenge akin to turning water into wine. From the most basic of ingredients the student flatter must create something edible, tasty, healthy and interesting – not to mention cope with the cooking ineptitudes of flatmates, most of whom have only two recipes in their repertoire – mince nachos and spaghetti bolognaise.

Since then, with budgets less constrained, and more exotic ingredients available, I have enjoyed inventing new dishes. Most have been delicious but inevitably there have been the recipes gone wrong. Everyone has experienced the disappointment of burnt, salt confused for sugar, failed to rise, or stuck in the pan cooking failures. Do not be disheartened: we must pick ourselves up, dust off the flour and try again, always searching for that next gastronomic sensation.

Over the last decade I've gained much experience in the world of food – from gourmet pizza girl, barista, café worker and deli diva to private home chef, caterer and café/bar manager. Secrets I have learned in the professional kitchen have helped refine my cooking methods, but essentially I am an everyday cook. My speciality is cooking in domestic kitchens with readily available and familiar ingredients, simple equipment and easily mastered skills. This is the essence of this book.

I love food. I have an unashamed passion for it. Above all, I love celebrating special events with special food. No matter what the occasion, good food can turn a pleasant experience into one remembered and talked about for years afterwards. These recipes are designed to help you create your own fabulous food stories and happy memories. I have also included hints for creating that special party ambience, and menu suggestions for many occasions. I hope this book will help you on your way to entertaining acclaim. Cook! Eat! And, most of all, enjoy!

Danielle Bowater

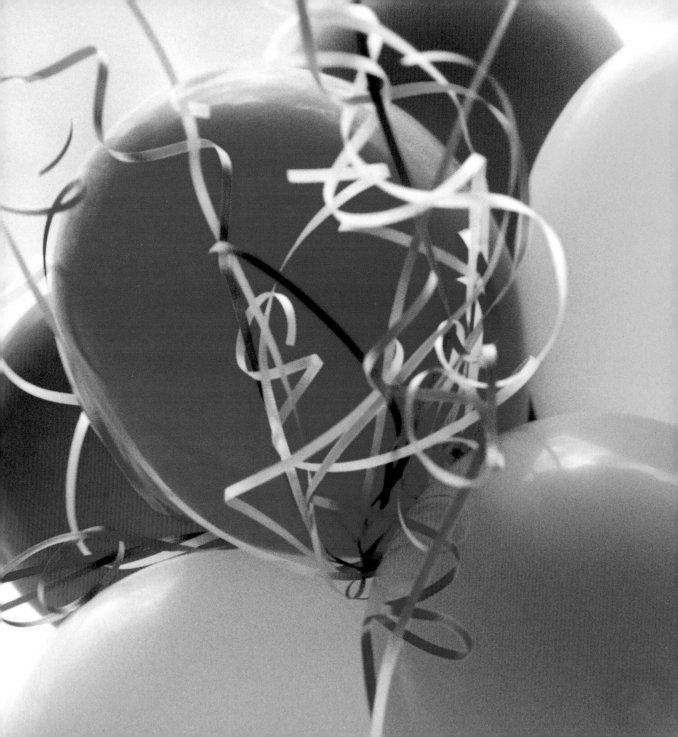

Party planning

A confession: once upon a time, my idea of party planning was sitting down a week beforehand with a stack of recipe books, deciding what to cook, then slinging around a few balloons and candles on the day. The food would be great but the atmosphere was, well, zilch. Then I wised up …

Setting the scene

When it comes to guests having a great time, atmosphere is almost as important as food and drink. It's a good idea to think about the style, setting, and perhaps theme, you want for a party before planning the menu. So – start early! Brainstorm. Steal ideas from magazines, restaurants, other parties you've enjoyed. Read the following pages and tick off the checklist.

Dress-ups and decorations

Themed parties can be a lot of fun and dress-ups help break the ice. I once catered a birthday party where the theme was 'Born in the Blitz'. The guests wore World War II clothes, and at one point an air-raid siren sent everyone fleeing to the basement, where Guinness stout was served. The party food was a plain, war-ration roast dinner, followed by apple pie. The event was a huge success.

Think about the atmosphere you want to create, and plan the decorations in advance. Simple touches make a big impact. Fresh colourful flowers cheer a room, tablecloths formalise an event, and balloons, banners and streamers add an exciting mardi gras feel.

An increasingly popular idea for special occasions such as birthdays and engagements is to create a display of photographs, old and new, of the guest (or guests) of honour. Everyone can contribute, adding their own captions and anecdotes.

Creature comforts

To ensure the party goes without a hitch, make sure you have:

Space
Keep open and uncluttered, for ease of movement. Remove precious things from harm's way.

Seating
Provide plenty of chairs, especially if it is a long event and/or older people will be present.

Dance floor
Nominate a space in advance where a spillage won't end in tears and heel marks won't leave permanent scars.

Heating and/or ventilation
Make sure it's at the right level. If the weather is cold, use safe heaters or an open fire with a screen. If it's hot or the party is crowded, switch on fans and open windows.

Citronella candles or mosquito coils
Set out a number if your event is outdoors and insects could be pesky.

Music

When it comes to party music, it's impossible to please all people all the time. My advice is to pick something you love and hope your enthusiasm rubs off on your guests.

Live music is fantastic if you have the budget. Try:

- a string quartet for a garden party
- a jazz ensemble for a swinging event
- an opera diva for a classy soirée
- DJs for a dance party

Chances are, though, that you'll be playing music through your stereo. Make sure your selection is at the ready and the volume is right. There's usually someone around who's eager to manage the music – just try and keep him or her to the play list!

If your party has a theme, choose matching music:

World music
African and Latin American music both have great party tempos, perfect for dancing.

Retro music
Pick a decade with guest-appeal.

Jazz, Dixie
Swing and be-bop create a languid, speakeasy ambience.

Motown
R 'n' B and soul are good for dancing.

Musicals
Chicago, *Porgy and Bess*, *The Rocky Horror Picture Show*, *Grease* and other well-known scores span the generation gap and get people in the mood.

Classical
Operatic love duets, famous piano sonatas and stirring symphonies enhance formal occasions.

Short of CDs?
Ask each guest to bring one, perhaps his or her all-time favourite. Or, even better, hire a karaoke machine – guaranteed to break the ice!

Lighting

Lighting is one of the best ways to create ambience. Flatter your guests with soft lighting, easily created with candles and lamps. Use fairy lights, strung around doorways or in trees, for a magical effect. Flares add drama to an outdoor setting, but ensure they're in a safe position. To highlight a pathway or entrance, try candles in jars.

Planning the menu

Your menu selection will be driven by the type of party you're giving. Take a look at the suggestions on pages 10–11. Give some thought, as well, to the time of year. In mid-winter, I love to serve plenty of hot, comforting food, accompanied by mulled wine. In sizzling summer, I emphasise cool, refreshing food and iced drinks.

Make the most of seasonal produce

Look around for fresh seasonal ingredients. Foods I particularly love using in-season are asparagus, an all too short treat, and summer fruits. Thanks to food importing and hot-house horticulture, it is now possible to get most fruit and vegetables 'fresh' year-round, but nothing tastes better than locally grown produce.

Go for variety

Even if you decide to serve only a small selection of foods, choose ones that offer a variety of texture, colour, flavour and shape. I have divided the book into 'food-type' chapters so it's easy to do this. For example, you may decide to serve one kind of dip, one kind of wrap and one kind of skewer.

Provide for food preferences

It's likely that some guests will have special dietary requirements, for example low-fat, low-carbohydrate, non-dairy, vegetarian or vegan. You could check with guests in advance, but it's probably sufficient to simply provide a selection of vegetarian, seafood, meat and poultry dishes, aiming for equal quantities of each. A vegetarian theme is always a safe bet: not only will it suit most guests, it's likely to be cheaper.

Cater for younger guests

If children or teenagers (or cautious adult eaters) are attending the party, remember to include some simple, unspiced food with recognisable and familiar ingredients. Cheesy tarts, pizzettas, sandwiches and suppli (risotto and mozzarella balls) are among the recipes that fit the bill.

Get the quantity right

Quantity depends on the length of the event, and whether it is being held in place of a meal. A general guideline is:

Two- to three-hour event – allow approximately 10 items per person, with three or four different types of food.

Meal-time event – allow approximately 15 items per person, with four or five different types of food.

Stay stress-free

Who wants to be stuck in the kitchen while there's fun to be had? Don't include too many recipes that need last-minute preparation or cooking – unless, of course, you have helpers on hand. Many of the recipes that follow can be made well in advance, and either served cold or readily reheated.

Menu suggestions

Chances are, your party is marking a special occasion – perhaps a birthday, anniversary, engagement or work promotion. Or maybe you're gathering to watch the big game, or just fancy having friends around. These sample menus provide a delightful medley of flavour and texture, with food appropriate to the occasion. They are, of course, only a guideline.

Sweet sixteen
Panini fingers 45
Cheesy tarts 58
Chocolate brownies 129 or Birthday cake
Retro fruit punch (non-alcoholic) 139

Twenty-first birthday
Pizzetta 46
Quesadilla 51
Spanakopita 72
Chicken skewers: Lime & ginger 91
    or Smoked paprika & yoghurt 92
Birthday cake
Retro fruit punch 139, beer, white wine & bubbles

Fiftieth birthday
Pissaladière with red pepper and olive 56
Suppli 80
Peking duck and mandarin pancakes 86
Bacon & prune skewers 94
Citrus or Summer fruit tarts 126
Birthday cake
White & red wine, and bubbles

Friday night drinks
Antipasti 26–33 or Cheeseboard 36
Long Island iced tea 140 & wine

Classy soirée
Wonton cups with Thai beef salad 55
Prawn balls 82, Dolmades 87 or Prawn skewers 93
Whitebait fritters 103 or Oysters 108
Berry ripple 128 or Chocolate pots 130
Feijoa-infused vodka with Ch'i 141, white wine & bubbles

Saturday night fever
Chilli orange pork pies 70
Samosas 74
Corn fritters with salsa 99
Beer-battered fish bites 107
Fortune cookies 125
Drunken melon 142, wine & beer

Boys' sports night
Dips 'n' dippers 16–23
Pizzetta 46
Pies: Potato-top 67 or Beef bourguignon 68
Beer

Office shout
Panini fingers 45
Chicken & apricot finger sandwiches 50
Cheesy tarts 58
Chocolate brownies 129
Orange juice, coffee & tea

Gals' night in

Crostini 48

Potato galettes with hot-smoked salmon & crème fraîche 60

Vietnamese spring rolls 79

Asparagus and prosciutto skewers 95

Margarita granita 143

Champagne cocktails 138

Themed menus

Themes are an excellent way of focussing food selection. I enjoy carrying a theme right through to drinks and decorations, creating an unusual and captivating atmosphere.

Love you long time (Asian)

Satay dip & roti 17

Salmon & wasabi cucumber cups 62

Pork & sesame balls 83

Peking duck with mandarin pancakes 86

Thai fish cakes 100 or Scallops on Asian coleslaw 111

Feijoa-infused vodka with Ch'i 141

Under the Tuscan sun (Mediterranean)

Selection of marinated olives and vegetables

Pizzetta 46 or Crostini 48

Spanakopita 72 or Dolmades 87

Suppli 80

Spanish fish cakes 102

Red wine

Kai moana (seafood)

Sushi 84

Fish cakes: Thai 100 or Spanish 102 or Whitebait fritters 103

Beer-battered fish bites 107

Oysters 108 or Grilled mussels 110

Scallops on Asian coleslaw 111

White wine

Gourmet green (vegetarian)

Beetroot dip with Turkish pide 19

Spanakopita 72 or Dolmades 87

Vietnamese spring rolls 79

Suppli 80

Corn fritters with salsa 99

Feijoa-infused vodka with Ch'i 141

Fire starter (spicy)

Quesadilla 51

Wonton cups with Thai beef salad 55

Chilli orange pork pies 70

Vietnamese spring rolls 79

Prawn balls 82 or Thai fish cakes 100

Beer

Presenting the food

The most gorgeous food can look abysmal if served badly. Conversely, plain food can look fantastic if imaginatively presented. When you're deciding which dishes to make, think about how you'll present them. You may even want to decide on serving platters first, and choose dishes to match.

Empty your cupboards of all your favourite platters and plates. Think about their shapes and colours. Classic white is always a safe choice, but who wants to be safe? Food looks stunning on coloured plates. My favourites are black, wasabi green, lemon yellow, burnt orange and fast-car red.

Red has been scientifically proven to stimulate the appetite, so if you use red plates be sure to over-cater. Vivid blue can also be amazing. In general I'm not a fan of patterned crockery but I have sometimes seen food on a busy, colourful platter look sensational.

If you're serving bread, hunt out large wooden trays, bowls or baskets, and line them with bright cloths or napkins.

Single-food platters

The easiest, most attractive way of serving party food is one type of food on a single platter. At stand-around parties, I like to serve a dish at a time so each can be savoured and enjoyed.

Mixed platters

Choose five or six different sorts of food, and arrange them together on a large platter. This is perfect for small, informal parties, or where guests are grouped around tables.

Buffet or tapas

Set platters of finger food casually on tables so guests can help themselves. You may also want to provide small plates, so guests can gather enough food to keep them going.

Petit-fours

Although it's usually associated with sweet treats, the classic petit-fours presentation can be happily applied to savoury finger food. Choose four interesting varieties, and serve one of each on individual plates. This is also great as an entrée for a formal seated dinner.

What you'll need

platters & plates – different shapes, sizes and colours

bowls & dishes – for dips, sauces and spreads

selection of glasses & cups – for some varieties of sweet treats

cheese knives, spreaders & spoons

skewers & toothpicks

napkins

Party checklist

Invitations

Compile a guest list and send out invitations. Include RSVP details. Advise of the dress code if you have one. There's nothing worse than turning up in jeans when everyone else is in Armani. Well, maybe not Armani, but you know what I mean.

Neighbours

If it's going to be a large, noisy affair, let them know well in advance!

Menu

Choose the recipes you want to make. Read them thoroughly to ensure there are no hidden surprises, and then create a shopping list.

Helpers

For formal parties, and those with a large number of guests, you may need extra help. Ask friends and family first. Assign them specific tasks or time slots so they can still take part in the festivities. If there are children or teenagers around, enlist them to pass around food. If you need to hire staff, try your local Student Job Search or professional agencies. Don't forget that there'll be clean-up afterwards too!

Props

Ensure you have all the necessary party props: equipment for serving food and drinks, music gear and decorations. Borrow from friends or hire to fill the gaps.

Shopping

Buy the best quality ingredients you can practicably source and reasonably afford.

Food

Prepare as much food as possible in advance. Only reheating and final assembly should be left until party day.

Set the scene

Move the furniture, hang the decorations, arrange the flowers, set up the candles.

Relax

Leave plenty of time to relax and get gorgeous before your guests arrive.

Party!

It's not just your guests who should be having a good time. Take time out to share their company and soak up the stunning food, drinks and atmosphere. They'll enjoy themselves more if you do.

Dips

Teaming dips and dippers is a simple way to feed guests at a casual or impromptu event. You can easily pick up pre-prepared foods from your local supermarket or deli, but home-made always tastes best. Here are some combinations I have found win favour every time.

Satay dip & roti 17

Hummus 18

Beetroot dip 19

Pita triangles 19

Guacamole 20

Salsa 21

Thai chilli dip 22

Pineapple & mint dip 22

Feta herb dip 23

Vegetable crudités 23

Satay dip & roti

This is a hot and spicy combination, perfect for cold winter evenings. The speedy satay dip can be made ahead of time and reheated. Authentic roti, a Malaysian-style unleavened bread, can be found in most supermarkets.

Satay dip

1 onion, finely diced

1 clove garlic, finely chopped

1 tablespoon vegetable oil

½ cup crunchy peanut butter

½ cup coconut cream

2 tablespoons soy sauce

3 tablespoons sweet Thai chilli sauce

In a small saucepan, sauté the onion and garlic in the oil until softened. Add the rest of the ingredients and simmer for 15 minutes.

Serve warm with the roti.

Roti

3 roti

vegetable oil, for frying

In a frying pan, heat 1 tablespoon of oil, or enough to cover the bottom of the pan, until quite hot. Fry each roti for 30 seconds on each side, or until crisp.

Cut roti into quarters and serve immediately (roti becomes very stodgy when cold).

Hummus

Hummus is a wonderful Turkish dish, now enjoyed worldwide. There are many ready-made varieties available, but making your own is super-easy and very cheap. This hummus will keep for a week in the refrigerator.

1 cup dried chick-peas, soaked overnight, or 300g (11oz) can chick-peas drained

½ cup tahini (sesame-seed paste)

juice of 1 large or 2 small lemons

1 teaspoon ground cumin

1 clove garlic

sea salt & freshly ground black pepper

2 tablespoons olive oil

¼ teaspoon cayenne pepper or paprika

If you're using dried chick-peas, soak them over-night and cook in plenty of unsalted water until they're very soft (about 1–1½ hours). Drain, reserving the cooking water. Allow to cool a little.

In a food processor, blend together the chick-peas, tahini, lemon juice, cumin and garlic. Add some reserved cooking water, or tap water, until the hummus is the desired consistency. Season to taste with salt and pepper.

Spoon the hummus into a bowl, drizzle with olive oil and dust lightly with cayenne pepper or paprika.

Serve with Turkish pide bread (now available in many supermarkets), pita triangles, or vegetable crudités (page 23).

Simply replace the tahini with one of the following for a simple variation on the traditional recipe:

1 cup mashed roast pumpkin

1 cup beetroot – canned or well-cooked

½–1 cup marinated sun-dried tomatoes

1 small aubergine – roasted whole in a moderate oven until soft. Remove the skin when cool and mash the flesh.

a whole bulb of garlic – drizzled with oil and roasted in a moderate oven until the garlic is soft – the pulp will easily squeeze out of the bulb.

Beetroot dip

I love the beautiful colour of beetroot. If using freshly cooked beetroot, try peeling them under running water to avoid pink fingers, or wear rubber gloves. An apron will protect any precious clothing!

425g well-cooked beetroot, peeled,
or 425g (15oz) can baby beets, drained

1 clove garlic

1 teaspoon cumin seeds, roasted & ground
with a mortar and pestle

1 teaspoon coriander seeds, roasted & ground

½ cup olive oil

¼ cup natural yoghurt

In a food processor or blender, combine the beetroot, garlic, spices and olive oil until smooth.

Place the dip in a bowl and swirl natural yoghurt on top.

Serve with pita triangles, Turkish pide bread or vegetable crudités (page 23).

Pita triangles

Eating uncooked pita bread is like eating a beer mat. It is well worth the effort of crisping it in the oven. Pita triangles are very versatile – they go with almost any dip and are a healthy alternative to potato chips.

4 pieces pita bread

olive oil, for brushing

Preheat the oven to 200°C/390°F.

Cut each pita into 6 or 8 triangles. Brush the triangles with olive oil and spread on a baking tray in a single layer. Bake until golden and crisp, about 10–15 minutes.

Serve the pita triangles while still warm.

Guacamole

There are endless recipes for guacamole. This one came from my mother, and every time I serve it my guests comment that it's the best they've ever tasted. Although it is not entirely authentic to use sweet Thai chilli sauce in a Mexican classic, the result is deliciously creamy and tasty.

2–3 tomatoes

1 ripe avocado, peeled & stoned

½ cup natural yoghurt or sour cream

1 garlic clove, crushed

1–2 tablespoons sweet Thai chilli sauce

juice of 1 lime

sea salt & freshly ground black pepper

To serve

corn chips

fresh coriander,

or 1 fresh chilli,

or sour cream & paprika

To peel the tomatoes, make criss-cross cuts on the top and bottom, place them in a bowl and cover with boiling water. Leave for 30 seconds, then tip out the water. Rinse them in cold water to cool. The skin should now peel easily away from the flesh. Cut each tomato in half. Squeeze out the juice and seeds, and discard the core at the top. Finely dice the tomatoes.

In a bowl, mash the avocado until smooth. Add all other ingredients, except the tomatoes, and mix well. Add the tomatoes and gently combine.

Spoon into a serving bowl, and decorate with coriander leaves, slices of fresh chilli, or a dollop of sour cream sprinkled with paprika.

Use the guacamole the same day, storing it in the refrigerator until ready to serve. To prevent dis-colouration, sprinkle with lime or lemon juice and cover with plastic wrap, pressing to make a seal on the top as a second skin.

Serve with any ready-made corn chips.

Salsa

In this recipe, I use a ready-made salsa as a basis. It's not only quick, but the resulting salsa has a great consistency and just the right balance of sweet, salt and tang. Salsa is a favourite among dieters as it is almost completely fat-free. It's also very refreshing, especially when served with vegetable crudités.

3 tomatoes

½ red onion

5cm piece cucumber

1 red, orange, green or yellow pepper

½ cup fresh coriander

juice of 1 lime

½ cup ready-made salsa, any flavour

To serve

corn chips,

or vegetable crudités

Cut each tomato in half. Squeeze out the juice and seeds, and discard the core at the top. Finely dice the tomatoes.

Finely dice the red onion, cucumber and pepper. Roughly chop the coriander.

Mix all ingredients in a bowl and let sit for at least one hour before serving so the flavours can mingle.

Serve with any ready-made corn chips, or with vegetable crudités (page 23).

I'm over onion soup and reduced cream dip and you probably are too. Here are two tasty alternatives, both quick and easy. Serve with your favourite potato chip – thick, plain salted are best. Bored with chips? Try rice crackers or vegetable crudités (opposite) as a healthy alternative.

Thai chilli dip

Dips cannot get simpler than this. You can even stir the sauce directly into the sour cream pottle – saving on dishes and making it easy to transport.

1 cup sour cream

2–4 tablespoons sweet Thai chilli sauce, to taste

In a bowl or pottle, mix the sour cream and sweet Thai chilli sauce.

Pineapple & mint dip

This seemingly odd combination is absolutely delicious. I consumed it by the bowlful, with chips and carrot sticks, during my high school exams. Nipping to the kitchen to prepare a study snack is an all-too-familiar way of procrastinating.

1 cup cream cheese

1 cup crushed pineapple, drained

½ cup mint, finely chopped

Start with cream cheese at room temperature, or soften it by microwaving on high for 30 seconds.

Place in a bowl with the pineapple and mint, and combine thoroughly.

Feta herb dip

This is a fresh, nutritious dip, and made with natural yoghurt it has a lot less fat than ready-made feta dips. I adore this dip and so do my friends – we find it perfect for snacking on while relaxing outdoors on long sunny days.

200g (7oz) feta

½ cup natural yoghurt or sour cream

1 small garlic clove

1 cup fresh herbs – mint, basil and/or parsley

For a different flavour, try replacing the herbs with cumin or fennel: dry-roast 1 tablespoon of either cumin seeds or fennel seeds in a frying pan, then crush them with a mortar and pestle.

Place all the ingredients in a food processor and blend until smooth.

Serve with Turkish pide bread, vegetable crudités (below), or pita triangles (page 19).

Vegetable crudités

Fresh, crunchy crudités can be made from a range of vegetables. Simply cut into small sticks or florets – enough to hold one good dollop of dip – and keep refrigerated, either in a bowl of cold water, with a bed of ice if you have it, or tightly wrapped in plastic.

carrot

celery

zucchini

cucumber

crisp salad leaves – such as chicory or cos lettuce

peppers – red, yellow, orange or green

snow peas – blanch by plunging into boiling water for 30 seconds, then refresh under cold running water

asparagus – blanch as for snow peas

broccoli, cauliflower or broccolini – blanch by plunging into boiling water for one minute, then refresh under cold running water

green beans – blanch as for broccoli

Antipasti

Antipasti is the classic Italian starter, and a perfect way to serve food at small casual gatherings – accompanied, of course, by a good red, Chianti-style wine. I really like the shared nature of antipasti. It's guaranteed to bring people together, and start lively food conversations.

The antipasti platter is not only beautiful and delicious – it's also quick and easy to create. Many alluring antipasti-style foods are now available in supermarkets, delicatessens and specialty food stores. I like to mix a bought selection with some home-made goodies.

When choosing what will go on your antipasti platter, think seasonally – include fresh fruits and vegetables in summer, and marinated and pickled vegetables in winter.

To serve, simply arrange your ingredients in piles on a platter or board. It can be a bit like creating a painting! I find that spreads and condiments are best served in little dishes (or try a halved capsicum), placed in the centre of the platter. Scatter the whole platter with torn basil leaves.

Mixed antipasti

Mix and match your favourite antipasti components from this list:

meats – salami, prosciutto, pastrami, cabanossi, chorizo, smoked chicken

seafood – smoked salmon, smoked mussels

fresh fruits and vegetables – cherry tomatoes, blanched asparagus or green beans, radishes, rock melon, figs, grapes, apples or pears, orange segments, feijoas, peaches

marinated and pickled vegetables – gherkins or cornichons, pickled onions, artichokes, caperberries, sun-dried tomatoes, slow-roasted tomatoes (page 29), roasted peppers (page 30), grilled zucchini or aubergine (page 31), marinated olives (page 32), marinated baby mushrooms (page 32)

cheese – fresh mozzarella, ricotta, grilled haloumi (page 28), baked feta (page 29), crumbled blue cheese, parmesan shavings

spreads and condiments – beetroot dip (page 19), feta herb dip (page 23), pesto or tapenade (page 33), caramelised onions (page 41), tomato chutney (page 41), cream cheese spread (page 49), blue cheese spread (page 49), paté, balsamic vinegar and extra virgin olive oil

toasted nuts – pine nuts, walnuts, almonds, macadamias (page 40)

breads – crostini (page 48), ciabatta, baguette, foccacia

Prosciutto antipasti

Prosciutto (also known as parma ham) is a salty, cured ham sliced paper-thin. It is now widely available, and is a very popular basis for antipasti, and deservedly so. Try it with one of these combinations:

fresh figs and blue cheese,

or pears, toasted walnuts, and blue cheese or parmesan shavings,

or peaches or rock melon, and mozzarella

Lay the prosciutto slices over a plate and casually arrange your chosen ingredients on top. Season with salt and freshly ground pepper, drizzle with extra virgin olive oil, and perhaps some balsamic vinegar, and scatter over a few torn basil leaves. Very impressive!

Make sure you take all of your antipasti ingredients out of the refrigerator well in advance. They'll be much more flavoursome served at room temperature.

Grilled haloumi

Haloumi is a traditional Greek-Cypriot white cheese, now available in most delicatessens and supermarkets. Some is even locally made. Composed of sheep's milk, goat's milk, or a combination of the two, haloumi is semi-firm and preserved in light brine.

200g (7oz) haloumi
1 tablespoon olive oil
sea salt & freshly ground black pepper

Slice the haloumi through the middle, then cut in half lengthways.

Fry the haloumi slices in the oil until golden brown, about two minutes each side. Season with salt and pepper.

Serve while hot and gooey.

Baked feta with lemon

200g (7oz) block of firm feta

zest of 1 lemon, coarsely grated

¼ cup olive oil

freshly ground black pepper

Preheat the oven to 220°C/425°F.

Slice the feta through the middle, then cut in half lengthways. Place the feta slices in an ovenproof dish lined with baking paper. Sprinkle with lemon zest and drizzle with olive oil. Season with pepper.

Bake for 15 minutes and serve while still warm.

Slow-roasted tomatoes

500g (18oz) tomatoes, red and ripe

¼ cup olive oil

sea salt & freshly ground black pepper

Preheat the oven to 120°C/230°F.

Cut the tomatoes in half. Place the tomato halves on a greased baking tray cut-side up. Sprinkle generously with salt and pepper.

Slowly roast for 4 hours. Set aside to cool.

Drizzle with oil. Refrigerated, they will last for a week.

Roasted peppers

3–4 peppers – red, orange and/or yellow
½ cup olive oil
½ cup balsamic vinegar
1 clove garlic, crushed
small handful basil, chopped
sea salt & freshly ground black pepper
¼ cup pine nuts, toasted (optional)

Cut the peppers in half, discard the seeds and membrane, and place under a hot grill, skin-side up, until charred and blistered. Set aside to cool.

Once cool enough to handle, peel and discard the skins. Slice into 2cm-wide strips.

Combine the oil, vinegar, garlic, basil, salt and pepper in a bowl. Whisk well.

Add the red pepper strips to the marinade. Cover and marinate for at least one hour before serving, turning occasionally. They will last refrigerated for a couple of weeks.

Sprinkle with pine nuts before serving if desired.

To toast the pine nuts, place them in a heavy-based frying pan and gently dry-roast. Once they start to brown, keep a close eye on them as they colour quickly.

Grilled zucchini or aubergine

4 medium zucchini, or 2 medium slender
aubergines
½ cup olive oil, plus extra for grilling/frying
juice of 2 lemons
1 garlic clove, crushed
small handful mint or basil, chopped
sea salt & freshly ground black pepper
½ cup feta, crumbled (optional)

Slice the zucchini or aubergines diagonally into
½cm-wide strips. If the aubergines are quite wide,
slice the strips in half lengthways as well.

Brush the zucchini or aubergine slices liberally
with oil, and grill or fry until nicely browned and
cooked through. Aubergines are thirsty and may
need more oil, but be sure to cook right through.
Set aside to cool.

In a bowl combine the oil, lemon juice, garlic, herbs,
salt and pepper. Whisk well.

Add the zucchini or aubergine slices to the lemon
juice mixture. Cover and marinate for at least one
hour before serving, turning occasionally. Refrigerated, this dish will last for a couple of weeks.

If desired, sprinkle with crumbled feta before
serving.

Marinated olives

3 cups black olives such as kalamata, with stone in

1 cup olive oil

1 lemon

3 cloves garlic, finely chopped

2 bay leaves

1 cinnamon quill

sea salt & freshly ground black pepper

Drain and rinse the olives in a colander.

Using a zester, make thin strips of lemon rind. If you don't have a zester, you can use a vegetable peeler instead – peel the lemon, being careful to leave behind the bitter white pith, and thinly slice the lemon peel with a knife.

Combine all ingredients in a bowl. Cover and marinate for at least two days before serving, turning occasionally. Refrigerated, the olives will last for months.

Marinated baby mushrooms

500g (18oz) baby mushrooms

½ cup olive oil

½ cup white wine vinegar

1 tablespoon caster sugar

3 cloves garlic, finely chopped

1 red chilli, deseeded and finely chopped

small handful parsley, chopped

sea salt & freshly ground black pepper

Wipe the mushrooms clean with a damp cloth or paper towel. Trim the stalks to the level of the cap and cut the mushrooms in half, through the stem.

Combine the oil, vinegar, sugar, garlic, chilli, parsley, salt and pepper in a bowl. Whisk well, until emulsified.

Add the mushrooms to the marinade. Cover and marinate for at least one hour before serving, turning occasionally. Refrigerated, they will last for a fortnight, with the flavour intensifying as time goes by.

Pesto

4 handfuls basil leaves

¼ cup pine nuts

¼ cup parmesan, grated

2 cloves garlic, finely chopped

½ cup olive oil

sea salt & freshly ground black pepper

Blend the basil, pine nuts, parmesan and garlic in a food processor. While the motor is running, slowly pour in the oil. Season with salt and pepper.

Tapenade

2 handfuls black olives, pitted

5 anchovy fillets

2 tablespoons capers

2 cloves garlic, finely chopped

¼ cup olive oil

sea salt & freshly ground black pepper

Blend all ingredients together in a food processor.

Cheeseboard

Cheeseboards are back in fashion, and rightly so. The growth of the New Zealand cheese industry and the ready availability of fantastic cheeses has made the modern cheeseboard a classy act.

Cheese is brilliant for 'drinks and nibbles' and a delicious alternative to dessert. Although there's a huge range of cheeses to choose from, and an equally daunting choice of accompaniments, creating a beautiful cheeseboard is remarkably easy.

Choosing cheeses

I recommend you buy local New Zealand cheeses – they are just superb. Three different cheeses will be enough to suit most people's tastes. Choose a variety of shapes, textures, colours and flavours. As a guide, select one from each of the following groups:

soft – brie, camembert

hard or semi-hard – cheddar, raclette, gruyere, havarti

something completely different – blue cheese (hard or soft), goat's cheese, feta, ricotta, mascarpone

Another approach is to select just one cheese – your absolute knock-out favourite – and serve simply, with an appropriate condiment.

Quantity

A good rule is to allow about 100 grams (3½ ounces) of cheese per person. If you're having a selection of three cheeses, allow about 30 grams (1 ounce) of each per person. I find the following an easy-to-remember guide:

cheeseboard for 4 – 125g (4½oz) of each cheese

cheeseboard for 8 – 250g (9oz) of each cheese

cheeseboard for 16 – 500g (18oz) of each cheese

Condiments & crackers

I like to match each cheese with a condiment. Here are some sublime partnerships:

blue cheese with honey walnuts or dried fig purée (opposite), fresh figs or sliced pears

brie or camembert with raisins in wine (page 40), roasted peppers (page 30), strawberries or grapes

cheddar with caramelised onions (page 41), relish, pickle, tomato chutney (page 41), sliced apples, gherkins, or thinly sliced prosciutto

goat's cheese with caramelised onions (page 41), or olives

feta with olives or roasted peppers (page 30)

mozzarella with figs, prosciutto, sliced pears or peaches

Serve the cheese with several different types of cracker, biscuit or bread that vary in texture, taste and appearance. Full-flavoured cheese will be best enjoyed with a plain water cracker or a fresh baguette.

Presentation

To bring out their full flavour and texture, cheeses and condiments should always be served at room temperature. This is absolutely vital for soft cheeses such as brie and camembert – I like to take them out of the refrigerator at least an hour in advance. Conversely, fresh fruit such as apples and pears should be sliced and added at the very last minute.

Place each cheese on a wooden board with its complimentary condiment next to it. Add crackers, biscuits or bread slices. Avoid using a crockery plate as a cheeseboard – it won't look as good, and the cheese knives may damage your good china.

Honey walnuts

½ cup walnut halves

2 tablespoons clear honey

Preheat the oven to 160°C/325°F.

Toast the walnut halves on a baking tray for 5–10 minutes. Allow to fully cool, and store in an air-tight container.

Serve in a small pile drizzled with clear honey. If your honey isn't runny enough to drizzle, simply microwave for 20 seconds, or place the jar in a bowl of hot water for a few minutes.

Dried fig purée

Spread on a cracker and teamed with blue cheese or a mature cheddar, this simple purée made from dried figs is delicious.

2 cups dried figs

½ cup water

juice of 1 lemon

1 tablespoon honey

2 teaspoons ground cardamom

Place the figs, half the water (¼ cup), lemon juice, honey and cardamom in a food processor. Blend until a spreadable paste is formed, adding the remaining water as necessary.

Raisins in wine

¼ cup raisins or sultanas
¼ cup white wine

Marinate the raisins in the wine for at least 8 hours, preferably overnight. Stored in a cool place, they will last for a fortnight.

Serve piled in a small bowl with a spoon.

Toasted nuts

Toasted nuts are infinitely superior to raw nuts. Simply toasting nuts in an oven maximises their flavour and crunch, as their aromatic oils are released.

1 cup shelled nuts – mixture selected from pistachios, cashews, brazils, walnuts, almonds and/or pecans
salt

Preheat oven to 160°C/325°F.

Spread the nuts in a single layer on a baking tray. You do not need to add any oil, as nuts contain their own.

Toast 5–10 minutes, tossing every few minutes, until lightly browned. The nuts will continue to brown slightly off the heat, so remove them from the baking sheet immediately. Spread them on a chopping board to cool.

Do not be alarmed if the nuts seem soft – as they cool they will dry and firm. Lightly salt, and serve in bowls.

Keep toasted nuts, when cooled, in an airtight container. Use within a fortnight.

Caramelised onions

3–4 onions, preferably red

2 tablespoons olive oil

2 tablespoons balsamic vinegar

1 tablespoon brown sugar

Halve the onions and slice into thin wedges, working from the centre outwards.

In a saucepan, combine the onions, oil, vinegar and brown sugar. Cook over a moderate heat, stirring occasionally, for 30–45 minutes until the onions are caramelised and tender. Add a little water if they start to stick to the saucepan.

Once the onions have cooled, transfer them into a preserving jar or lidded container, and store them in the refrigerator.

Tomato chutney

500g (18oz) tomatoes, quartered and deseeded

1 onion, finely sliced

2 cooking apples, peeled, cored and finely sliced

6 tablespoons brown sugar

1 teaspoon mustard seeds

2 cloves

½ cinnamon quill

2 pinches salt

¼ cup water

¼ cup balsamic vinegar

pinch chilli powder (optional)

In a saucepan, combine the tomatoes, onion, apples and brown sugar. Cook over a moderate heat, stirring occasionally, until thickened.

Add the mustard seeds, cloves, cinnamon, salt, water and vinegar, stirring well to combine. Also add a pinch of chilli powder if desired.

Simmer, covered, for 1–1½ hours, stirring occasionally, until a chutney texture is achieved. Add a little water if the chutney starts to stick to the saucepan.

Store the chutney in preserving jars, or any container with a lid. Once it has cooled, keep it in the refrigerator.

Bread

Canapés based on bread are a good choice at events where a lot of alcohol will be consumed, because they are more substantial than many other finger foods. They are particularly suited to occasions such as 18th and 21st birthday parties, where younger drinkers, often with hearty appetites, will be in attendance.

Panini fingers

Mini-panini are now readily available from many bakeries, although I still prefer to use regular-sized panini cut into fingers – they are less fiddly and the cut edge nicely displays the filling. Two classic fillings are given below, but you can fill the panini with just about any favourite filling.

4 panini (or 16 mini-panini)

fillings (below)

1 tablespoon oil

white paper napkins or baking paper

Preheat a flat or ribbed sandwich press. Brush with oil.

Cut the panini in half through the middle and fill with your chosen filling(s). Toast until golden brown. Set aside to cool to room temperature.

Cut regular-sized panini into 4 fingers. Wrap each panini finger with a white paper napkin or a strip of baking paper, and arrange on a plate with the paper join hidden on the underside.

....

Ham & cheese filling

4 slices ham-on-the-bone

1½ cups cheddar cheese or mozzarella, grated

½ cup tomato chutney (page 41) or relish

A slice of ham, a sprinkle of cheese and a slather of relish per panini, and you're done.

Roast vegetable & pesto filling

2 zucchini, sliced lengthways into ½ cm strips

2 red peppers, cut into eighths

2 field mushrooms, thickly sliced

¼ cup olive oil

sea salt & freshly ground black pepper

1½ cups cheddar cheese or mozzarella, grated or thinly sliced

½ cup pesto (page 33)

Preheat the oven to 180°C/350°F.

Place the vegetables in an ovenproof dish. Drizzle with oil and season with salt and pepper. Bake for 20 minutes, until the vegetables are softened.

Spread on pesto, layer with roasted vegetables, and sprinkle with cheese.

Pizzetta

When I worked in a pizza outlet as an after-school job, not only did I learn to drive like a pro, I learnt to love making and eating pizza. Use this recipe to make any size pizza you like. A walnut-sized piece of dough makes a pizza base about five centimetres in diameter, a peach-sized piece makes one of about 10 centimetres. In an informal setting make large pizzas and serve as slices.

Pizza dough

3½ cups (400g/14oz) strong white flour

1 cup lukewarm water

1 tablespoon olive oil

1 tablespoon dried yeast

½ teaspoon sugar

½ teaspoon salt

Use mini pita breads as an alternative to making your own pizza dough.

Preheat the oven to 220°C/425°F.

Place all ingredients in a food processor, or a cake mixer with a dough hook. Mix together and let the machine knead the dough on low speed for about 10 minutes, until smooth and elastic. You can mix the dough by hand of course, but it will need a good 15 minutes of kneading.

Transfer the pizza dough to a greased bowl. Cover with plastic wrap or a tea towel and allow to rise in a warm, draught-free place until doubled in size – about 1½ hours.

Knock back the dough and allow it to rise again, covered, for a further 30 minutes.

To make the bases, start by breaking off a piece of dough, walnut- to peach-sized. On a lightly oiled surface, roll in a circular motion to form a ball. Transferring to a well-floured bench, roll the dough out as thinly as possible with a rolling pin.

Place the bases on to a baking paper-lined baking tray, leaving a one centimetre gap between each. Top with your chosen toppings and bake for 10–20 minutes, depending on size, until crisp and golden.

Serve hot or at room temperature.

Pizzetta toppings

Get creative with your pizza toppings, or try one of my favourites below. I've listed the ingredients in the order in which they should be put on the base. Season generously with sea salt & freshly ground black pepper.

potato & rosemary – very thinly sliced raw potato, crushed garlic, fresh rosemary and grated parmesan

Pacific – tomato chutney (page 41) or relish, ham, pineapple and grated mozzarella

blue – caramelised onions (page 41), prosciutto, sliced fresh figs and blue cheese

margarita – tomato chutney (page 41) or relish, basil leaves, grated mozzarella and grated parmesan

salmon – cream cheese spread (page 49), smoked salmon, chopped dill or grated lemon zest, and capers or caperberries

Sicilian – tomato chutney (page 41) or relish, baby spinach leaves, roasted red pepper, sliced field mushrooms, grated mozzarella and grated parmesan

mushroom – caramelised onions (page 41), sliced field mushrooms, fresh or dried thyme and crème fraîche

Spanish – tomato chutney (page 41) or relish, sliced fried chorizo (spicy Spanish sausage), feta, fresh or dried oregano and grated mozzarella

Greek – pesto (page 33), thinly sliced red onion, cherry tomatoes, feta and grated mozzarella

Italian – pesto (page 33), slow-roasted tomatoes (page 29), anchovies, olives, grated mozzarella and grated parmesan

Crostini

Crostini, literally 'little crusts', are fantastically versatile. There are an infinite number of toppings and they are suitable for any type of party. To help you on your way I've given some suggestions and recipes, but feel free to experiment, or simply pop into your local deli for some spreads or patés.

1 loaf baguette or ciabatta, preferably at least a day old

½ cup olive oil

sea salt & freshly ground black pepper

selection of toppings

Preheat the oven to 140°C/275°F.

Slice the loaf into half-centimetre slices.

In a small bowl, mix the oil with a generous pinch of salt and pepper. Brush both sides of each bread slice liberally with the oil mixture.

Spread the slices on a baking tray and bake for 15–20 minutes, turning over once. The crostini should be completely dry and crispy, and only slightly browned.

When the crostini are cool, store them in an airtight container. They will last a couple of weeks; if they become a little stale, refresh in a warm oven.

When ready to eat, top with your favourite topping(s) and serve immediately.

Crostini toppings

cream cheese spread (opposite), smoked salmon, sprinkled with chopped dill or capers

blue cheese spread (opposite), toasted walnut halves and capers

pesto (page 33) with slow-roasted tomatoes (page 29) and parmesan shavings

tapenade (page 33) with roasted peppers (page 30)

red pepper & walnut spread (opposite) with basil leaves

hummus (page 18) with pitted olives, drizzled with extra virgin olive oil

feta & herb dip (page 23) with grilled zucchini or aubergine (page 31) and mint leaf

paté with sliced gherkin

Bread spreads

These simple spreads can be used in many ways – on crostini, pizzetta, fresh and toasted sandwiches. Use them on their own, or as a basis for a special topping or filling.

Red pepper & walnut spread

3 red peppers

1 cup walnuts, toasted and chopped

2 cloves garlic

sea salt & freshly ground black pepper

Cut the peppers in half, discard the seeds and membrane, and place under a hot grill, skin-side up, until charred and blistered. Set aside to cool. Once cool enough to handle, peel and discard the skins.

Toast the walnuts in an oven for 5–10 minutes at 160°C/325°F.

Blend all ingredients together in a food processor. Add a little olive oil if the mixture is too thick.

Blue cheese spread

½ cup cream cheese, room temperature

½ cup blue cheese, crumbled

¼ cup dry white wine

Place the cream cheese in a bowl. Add the blue cheese and white wine, and combine thoroughly.

Cream cheese spread

1 cup cream cheese, room temperature

¼ cup white wine

juice of 1 lemon

Place the cream cheese in a bowl. Add the white wine and lemon juice, and combine thoroughly.

For extra flavour add chopped anchovies, capers and/or crushed garlic.

Chicken & apricot finger sandwiches

makes 12 fingers or 16 triangles

I've been disappointed by many a flaccid or over-margarined finger sandwich. This is the best finger sandwich I have found. Sandwiches are best made fresh on the day. If this isn't possible, cover them with shredded iceberg lettuce, wrap in plastic and refrigerate.

8 slices white or multigrain bread, sandwich-sliced

3 whole peppercorns

1 bay leaf

1 skinless chicken breast

1 stick celery, finely chopped

1 small clove garlic, crushed

½ cup mayonnaise (below)

sea salt & freshly ground black pepper

3 ripe apricots, thinly sliced, or salad greens

Pour 2 cups of water into a saucepan, along with the peppercorns, bay leaf and chicken breast, and bring to the boil. Simmer, with the lid on, for 5 minutes. Leave the chicken in the poaching liquid to cool for 15 minutes.

Pat the chicken dry with paper towel and finely dice. Mix together the chicken, celery, garlic, mayonnaise, salt and pepper. Keep refrigerated until ready to use.

Lay out 4 slices of bread. Spread a quarter of the mixture on each slice. Top with the thin slices of ripe apricot or salad greens, and finally with the remaining bread slices.

With a bread knife, trim off the crusts and cut the sandwiches into fingers (thirds) or triangles.

....

Mayonnaise

1 egg

1 pinch sugar

1 pinch salt

1 pinch pepper, preferably white

1 cup vegetable oil

In a food processor, blend together all ingredients, using only one-third of the oil. When this mixture has emulsified, slowly drizzle in the remaining oil with the motor running. Adjust seasoning to taste.

Other sandwich filling ideas:

chicken and thinly sliced avocado

smoked salmon, cream cheese spread (page 49) and thinly sliced cucumber

salami, cream cheese spread (page 49) and thinly sliced gherkins

mashed boiled egg, mixed with chopped parsley and mayonnaise, with thinly sliced ham or tomato

prosciutto, blue cheese spread (page 49) and thinly sliced ripe figs

canned tuna, chopped spring onions, grated lemon zest, mayonnaise and salad greens

....

Quesadilla

makes 18 triangles

A quesadilla is a Mexican toasted sandwich – perfect when partnered with a jug of margarita or sangria!

6 tortillas, ready-made

1 cup cheddar cheese, grated

6 tablespoons sweet Thai chilli sauce

sea salt & freshly ground black pepper

vegetable oil, for frying

Lay out 3 tortillas and divide the cheese and chilli sauce between them. Season with salt and pepper, and cover with the remaining tortillas.

Fry each quesadilla on its own in a non-stick frying pan, brushed with oil, until golden on both sides.

Cut each quesadilla into 6 triangles. Serve warm.

Try these filling variations:

guacamole (page 20) or sliced avocado

salsa (page 21) or sliced tomato and red onion

fresh coriander, roughly chopped

grilled aubergine slices

refried beans

jalapeno chilli, finely chopped

Tarts

Tarts come in many forms – cases with pastry, potato, noodles, bread or wonton wrappers, and any filling imaginable. Take advantage of the opportunity for drama in presentation that tart cases provide. Use colour and texture to full effect. Guests will be very impressed – tarts look like more work than they actually are.

Wonton cups with Thai beef salad

makes 24

Wonton cups make for easy presentation and consumption of what would normally be impossible to eat as finger food – salad. I've selected Thai beef salad for the filling as it is my favourite Asian salad. Wonton wrappers are available from Asian food stores.

Wonton cups

24 wonton wrappers

2 tablespoons peanut oil

The cases can be made several days ahead and stored in an airtight container.

Preheat the oven to 180°C/350°F.

Cut rounds from the wonton wrappers using 5cm cookie cutters. Brush the rounds with peanut oil and push them into 24 mini-muffin tins. Bake for 5 minutes or until crispy. Allow to cool on wire racks.

To serve, fill each wonton cup with a teaspoonful of salad, artfully place a marinated beef strip on top of the salad and sprinkle with a few chopped peanuts. Serve immediately.

Thai beef salad

500g (18oz) beef fillet steak

½ cup coriander, finely chopped

1 fresh red chilli, deseeded & finely chopped

juice of 1 lime

1 dash fish sauce

1 teaspoon brown sugar

1 ripe red tomato

2cm piece telegraph cucumber

1 spring onion, halved lengthways & finely chopped

¼ cup roasted peanuts, chopped

Fry the steak until medium-rare – about 2 minutes each side, turning only once. Set aside to rest for 10 minutes, then slice widthways into half-centimetre wide strips.

In large bowl, make the marinade by mixing together the coriander, chilli, lime juice, fish sauce and brown sugar. Toss the beef strips into the bowl, and marinate for at least 30 minutes, but preferably overnight.

To make the salad, cut the tomato in half, remove the core, squeeze out the seeds and finely dice. Deseed and finely dice the cucumber. Halve the spring onion lengthwise and finely chop. Mix gently.

Pissaladière with red pepper & olive

makes 24 patty tin, or 48 mini-muffin tin tarts

Pissaladière is a classic onion and tomato tart originating from Provençe. I've been eating and enjoying family-sized pissaladières for years. I first prepared them mini-sized for a party, and they were so successful I've been making them regularly ever since.

For the filling

500g (18oz) ripe, red tomatoes

50g (2oz) butter

3 red onions, finely chopped

1 teaspoon fresh thyme leaves, or dried thyme

3 anchovies, chopped (optional)

1 tablespoon tomato paste

1 teaspoon fresh oregano leaves, or dried oregano

2 pinches sugar

1 pinch chilli powder

4 tablespoons parmesan, grated

sea salt & freshly ground black pepper

When nice ripe red tomatoes are hard to come by, I have successfully made this tart with tinned Italian tomatoes instead. Use a 400g (14oz) can of whole peeled tomatoes: drain, remove the cores at the top of the tomatoes, and squeeze out the excess liquid from the tomatoes using your hands. Chop and use as per the recipe.

To peel the tomatoes, make criss-cross cuts on the top and bottom, place them in a bowl and cover with boiling water. Leave for 30 seconds, then tip out the water. Rinse them in cold water to cool. The skin should now peel easily away from the flesh. Cut each tomato in half and squeeze out the seeds. Discard the core at the top and finely dice the tomato.

Melt the butter in a frying pan and add the onions, thyme and anchovies (optional). Sauté until the onions are transparent and soft. Remove the onions to a bowl and set aside.

In the same frying pan, add the diced tomato, tomato paste, oregano, sugar and chilli powder. Cook gently for 15 minutes, or until excess moisture has evaporated. Add the tomato mixture to the onions and mash together with a wooden spoon. Stir in the parmesan and season with salt and pepper. Allow to cool.

Making the tarts

3 sheets of pre-rolled short savoury pastry

12 or 24 black olives

roasted red pepper (page 30)

Preheat the oven to 200°C/390°F. Grease mini-muffin or patty tins by spraying or brushing with oil.

Cut out rounds of pastry using pastry cutters, or an upturned drinking glass and sharp knife – the rounds should be large enough so that the edge of the pastry will come right to the top of the tin. Push the pastry rounds into the tins and prick the base a few times with a fork, to reduce puffing.

Using a teaspoon, fill the tart cases almost to the top with the tomato filling.

Bake in the oven for about 15 minutes until brown.

Halve the black olives and remove the stones with a sharp knife. Garnish the top of each tart with half a black olive and a strip of roasted red pepper.

Serve either warm or at room temperature.

You can make these tarts the day before you wish to serve them. Store the cooled tarts, pre-garnish, in an airtight container. Reheat in a warm oven if desired.

Cheesy tarts

These cheesy tarts are perfect for morning and afternoon teas, especially office shouts. Make them the day before, and when they are fully cooled store them in an airtight container. They're quick to reheat. Here are two simple, economical fillings, but you can easily adapt the recipes to suit your taste.

Corn, bacon & cheese filling

410g (14oz) creamed corn

4 rashers streaky bacon

1 onion

1 cup cheddar cheese, grated

1 egg

pinch nutmeg, ground or freshly grated

sea salt & freshly ground black pepper

Fry or grill the bacon until crispy. Set to cool on paper towels to remove excess grease. When cool, chop the bacon into little pieces (scissors make this easy).

Finely dice the onion, and soften by gently sautéeing in a frying pan, or microwaving on high for 2 minutes.

Mix all ingredients in a bowl, seasoning with salt and pepper.

Spinach & cheese filling

700g (25oz) fresh spinach or 300g (10oz) packet frozen spinach, well thawed

1 onion, finely diced

250g (9oz) ricotta or cottage cheese

1 cup grated cheddar cheese

1 egg

pinch nutmeg, ground or freshly grated

sea salt & freshly ground black pepper

Prepare the fresh spinach: wash thoroughly to remove any grit, cut off any tough stalks, and wilt in a frying pan on a gentle heat – this will only take a few minutes. Drain in a colander, and when cool, squeeze out as much liquid as you can with your hands. For frozen spinach, once thawed, drain and squeeze out excess liquid.

Soften the onion by gently sautéeing in a frying pan or microwaving on high for 2 minutes.

Mix all ingredients in a bowl, seasoning with salt and pepper.

Making the tarts

3 sheets pre-rolled flaky, puff or
short savoury pastry

¼ cup chives or parsley, chopped

Ready-made pastry makes these tarts super-easy.
I prefer to use flaky, even though it can
make for a messy floor during consumption!

As an alternative to pastry, use sandwich-sliced
white, wholemeal or wholegrain bread. Cut
bread rounds using cookie cutters or scissors.
Brush liberally with oil or melted butter.

Preheat the oven to 200°C/390°F. Grease mini-muffin or patty tins by spraying or brushing with oil.

Cut out rounds of pastry using pastry cutters, or an upturned drinking glass and sharp knife – the rounds should be large enough so that the edge of the pastry will come right to the top of the tin. Push the pastry rounds into the tins and prick the base a few times with a fork, to reduce puffing.

Using a teaspoon, fill the tart cases almost to the top with your chosen filling.

Bake in the oven for 15–20 minutes until browned. Do not be alarmed if the filling puffs up; it will drop when cooled.

Decorate by sprinkling with chopped chives or parsley.

Let the tarts cool a little before serving so as not to burn any mouths with the hot cheesy filling.

Potato galettes with hot-smoked salmon & crème fraîche

Serve these galettes as the party starts – they make a terrific first impression and are the perfect accompaniment to a glass of bubbles. If your guests are hesitant to tuck in, or arrive in dribs and drabs, it doesn't matter if the cases cool a little. You can also make them with filo pastry.

200g (7oz) hot-smoked salmon

finely grated zest and juice of 1 lemon

sea salt & freshly ground black pepper

6–8 small waxy potatoes

½ cup crème fraîche

chives, for decoration

If you're wondering what the difference is between hot-smoked and cold-smoked salmon – here is a simple answer. Hot-smoked salmon is cured in a wet brine and smoked at a high temperature, resulting in an opaque, flaky texture and pale orange colour. Cold-smoked salmon is cured in a dry brine and smoked at a low temperature, resulting in a translucent, soft texture and bright orange colour.

Make the filling at least one hour before you wish to serve the galettes, to optimise the lemony flavour.

Lightly fork together the salmon, lemon zest and juice in a bowl, and season generously with salt and pepper. Set aside.

Preheat the oven to 200°C/390°F.

Grease 24 mini-muffin tins (or 12 standard patty tins) thoroughly to prevent the starch in the potatoes sticking to the tins.

Slice the potatoes as thinly as possible, using a Chinese mandolin slicer if you happen to have one. Line the tins with 5 potato slices overlapping each other, in each hollow. Firmly push together the layers with your fingers.

You can make the galette cases up to 3 days in advance. Reheat them before serving. Refrigerated, the filling will also keep for 3 days, but make sure you let it return to room temperature before serving. However, once the galettes have been filled, do serve them immediately.

Bake the potato galettes in the oven for 15–20 minutes, until the layers have joined and the edges are brown and crispy. Allow to cool a little, then carefully remove them from the tin.

Fill the warm galette cases with a dessertspoonful of salmon filling, and top with a teaspoonful of crème fraîche and a criss-cross of chives.

Filo cases with salmon

6–8 sheets filo pastry
olive oil

Preheat the oven to 180°C/350°F.

Cut the filo into 10cm squares (this will make about 24 cases). Brush each sheet of filo pastry with oil. Fold twice into a 4-layered, 5cm square. Push the filo into mini-muffin tins.

Bake the cases for about 10 minutes, until lightly browned and crispy.

Fill the cases the same way as for the potato galettes.

Salmon & wasabi cucumber cups

Cucumber cups are light and refreshing, perfect for a summer party. I like to think of these cups as inside-out sushi, although there is not a grain of rice in sight.

1 long slender telegraph cucumber, approximately 4 cm in diameter

12 small, thin slices of smoked salmon

¼ sheet nori, very finely shredded

¼ cup sesame seeds, toasted

wasabi mayonnaise (opposite)

Prepare the cucumber cups no more than one hour before serving. Cover them with plastic wrap and keep them in the refrigerator so they don't dry out. Serve immediately once filled.

Slice the cucumber into 15mm rounds. Using a pastry cutter, create rounds out of each slice of cucumber, removing the skin. If you haven't the right size pastry cutter, trim off the cucumber skin with a knife, making sure you get a nicely rounded result.

Using a melon-baller or teaspoon, make a small hollow in the top of each round to form a cup.

Fill each cucumber cup with a one teaspoonful of wasabi mayonnaise and top with an artfully placed piece of smoked salmon.

For decoration, sprinkle half the cups with the finely shredded nori, and the other half with toasted sesame seeds (they can be gently browned in a heavy-based frying pan).

Wasabi mayonnaise

1 egg

1 tablespoon lemon juice

1 cup vegetable oil

1 tablespoon wasabi

sea salt & freshly ground black pepper

This wasabi mayonnaise can be prepared
up to a day in advance.

In a food processor, blend together the egg, lemon juice and one-third of the oil. When this mixture has emulsified, slowly drizzle in the remaining oil with the motor running. Add the wasabi and season with salt and pepper.

Small pies

Pies are the essential finger food for events where blokes are in attendance, especially watching the big game. They are great with beer, or served as comfort food in winter with warming red wine. The beauty of pies is that you can prepare them in advance, and simply reheat while enjoying a relaxed drink.

Potato-top pies

A classic kiwi pie for the classic kiwi bloke or sheila.

2 tablespoons oil

1 onion, finely diced

2 cloves garlic, finely chopped

500g (18oz) beef mince

4 tablespoons tomato sauce

2 tablespoons Worcestershire sauce

sea salt & freshly ground black pepper

3 sheets pre-rolled savoury short pastry

4–5 large floury potatoes, peeled and quartered

1 tablespoon butter

milk

salt

½ cup cheddar cheese, grated

To quickly thaw pre-rolled pastry sheets, spread them out on a wire rack. Keep the pastry covered and cool until ready to use.

To make the beef filling, start by frying the onion and garlic in the oil until softened. Add the beef mince and brown, breaking up with a wooden spoon. Stir in the tomato and Worcestershire sauces and season with salt and pepper. Set aside.

For the topping, cook the potatoes in boiling salted water until soft, about 15 minutes. Drain and then return to the hot pan to dry. Mash the potatoes with the butter and enough milk to form a firm, yet creamy, mash. Season generously with salt.

To make the pies, preheat the oven to 200°C/390°F. Grease 24 standard size patty tins.

Cut out 24 rounds of pastry using pastry cutters, or an upturned drinking glass and a knife, and push into the patty tins – the pastry should come right to the top of the tin. Prick the pastry base a few times with a fork, to reduce puffing.

Using a teaspoon, fill the pie bottoms with the meat filling. Cover each pie with a generous blob of mashed potato. Sprinkle with grated cheese.

Bake in the oven for 15 minutes or until browned. Serve warm.

Beef bourguignon pies

The classic French casserole beef bourguignon, served with potato gratin, is one of my mother's favourite winter meals for entertaining. I first made these pies when she had some leftovers. They were so incredibly rich and tasty I have now adapted the recipe specifically for a small-chunk pie.

For the filling

2 rashers bacon

1 onion, finely chopped

500g (18oz) beef steak, 1cm dice

2 tablespoons flour

1 cup red wine

1 cup beef stock

1 clove garlic, finely chopped

1 strip of orange zest

2 bay leaves

5 parsley stalks

1 sprig fresh thyme (or 2 teaspoons dried thyme)

1 cup tiniest baby mushrooms, quartered

1 tablespoon butter

sea salt & freshly ground black pepper

As pies were invented to use up last night's leftovers, feel free to use any leftovers you may have – casseroles, stews, tagines, curries, roast meat/poultry, vegetables and gravy – in place of the beef bourguignon.

In a heavy-based saucepan, fry the bacon until crisp and brown. Remove and finely chop. Set aside. In the same saucepan, fry the onion in the bacon fat until golden. Set aside with the bacon.

Return the saucepan to the heat, and keeping the temperature high, fry half the beef until golden brown (frying over a high heat, in two batches, will prevent the beef from stewing and becoming chewy). Remove and set aside. Fry the remaining half of the beef and set aside.

Pour off any fat and discard. Return the beef to the pan and add 1 tablespoon of flour and turn the heat to high. Let the flour cook a little and, still on high heat, add the red wine. Cook for 5 minutes.

Make a bouquet garni by tying together the orange zest, bay leaves, parsley and thyme with a piece of string. Add the bacon, onions, bouquet garni, garlic and stock to the beef. Simmer, covered, for 30 minutes. Add the mushrooms and simmer for another 30 minutes.

Mix together the remaining tablespoon of flour and the tablespoon of butter until a paste is formed. Remove ½ cup of liquid from the pan and mix in the flour/butter mixture. Return to the pan and bring the casserole to the boil. Simmer until thickened.

Allow to cool.

Making the pies

5 sheets pre-rolled puff, flaky
or savoury short pastry

1 egg, beaten

Preheat the oven to 200°C/390°F. Grease 24 standard size patty tins.

Cut out 24 rounds of pastry using pastry cutters, or an upturned drinking glass and a knife, and push into the patty tins – the pastry should come right to the top of the tin. Prick the pastry base a few times with a fork, to reduce puffing. Cut another 24 pastry rounds for the pie tops – these should be slightly smaller than the pie bottoms.

Using a teaspoon, fill the pie bottoms with the beef filling. Cover each pie with a pastry top and firmly press together the edges. Prick the pie tops a couple of times with a fork. Brush with beaten egg for a glossy finish.

Bake in the oven for about 15 minutes, or until browned. Serve warm.

Chilli orange pork pies

makes 24 patty tin pies

These delicious pies are a Bowater family tradition and remind me of many happy Christmases past. No one in my immediate family likes Christmas fruit mince pies, so we make these spicy pies instead. A plate of pies is reheated for every holiday visitor, and served with some extra sweet Thai chilli sauce for dipping.

For the filling

2 tablespoons oil

1 orange, thin strips of zest finely chopped

1 onion, finely diced

500g (18oz) pork mince

½ cup carrot, kumara, parsnip or zucchini, grated

sea salt & freshly ground black pepper

2–3 tablespoons sweet Thai chilli sauce, plus extra, to serve

In a frying pan, brown the orange zest in the oil – this can happen quickly so keep an eye on it. Add the onion and cook until softened. Add the pork mince and brown, breaking it up with a wooden spoon.

Add your chosen grated vegetable to the mince and cook until softened. This will keep the filling moist.

Stir in the salt and pepper, and chilli sauce, to taste.

Making the pies

5 sheets pre-rolled puff, flaky or
short savoury pastry

1 egg, beaten

These pies will keep for one week. Simply store in the
refrigerator when completely cooled, and reheat
when needed.

Preheat the oven to 200°C/390°F. Grease 24 standard size patty tins.

Cut out 24 rounds of pastry using pastry cutters, or an upturned drinking glass and a knife, and push into the patty tins – the pastry should come right to the top of the tin. Prick the pastry base a few times with a fork, to reduce puffing. Cut another 24 pastry rounds for the pie tops – these should be slightly smaller than the pie bottoms.

Using a teaspoon, fill the pie bottoms with the meat filling. Cover each pie with a pastry top and firmly press together the edges. Prick the pie tops a couple of times with a fork. Brush with beaten egg for a glossy finish.

Bake in the oven for about 15 minutes or until browned. Serve warm.

Spanakopita

Many people are put off cooking with filo pastry as it has a reputation for being a little difficult. Do not fear: just remember to keep the pastry covered with a damp, clean tea towel until ready to use.

For the filling

700g (25oz) fresh spinach or 300g (10oz) packet frozen spinach, well thawed

200g (7oz) feta, mashed with a fork

½ cup parmesan, grated

1 clove garlic, crushed

¼ cup parsley, finely chopped

¼ cup basil, finely chopped

1 egg, beaten

2 tablespoons pine nuts, toasted (page 30)

freshly ground black pepper

Use samosa filling (page 74) as an alternative to spinach and feta filling.

Prepare the fresh spinach: wash thoroughly to remove any grit, cut off any tough stalks, and wilt in a frying pan on a gentle heat – this will take only a few minutes. Drain in a colander, and when cool, squeeze out as much liquid as you can with your hands. For frozen spinach, once thawed, drain and squeeze out excess liquid. Chop the spinach roughly.

In a bowl, combine the spinach, feta, parmesan, garlic, parsley, basil, egg and pine nuts. Combine thoroughly and season with pepper.

Making the spanakopita

16 sheets filo pastry

½ cup oil

¼ cup sesame seeds

To make the triangles, start by preheating the oven to 180°C/350°F.

Take 2 filo pastry sheets at a time, keeping the remaining sheets covered with a damp tea towel. Brush oil on one of the sheets and lay the other on top. Cut the sheets lengthways into three long strips – scissors work well.

At the top of each piece of filo pastry, place about a tablespoonful of filling. Fold over the right-hand corner to meet the opposite side, then fold over towards you. Fold over the left-hand corner to meet the opposite side, then fold over towards you. Keep repeating this process until you reach the end of the strip of filo pastry.

Seal the triangle parcel by brushing with oil, and paint the whole triangle with oil. Place on a baking tray lined with baking paper.

Repeat with the rest of the filo pastry and the spinach filling.

Sprinkle the filo triangles with untoasted sesame seeds. Bake for 10–15 minutes, or until golden brown.

Serve while still hot and crispy.

Samosas

Crispy, puffed deep-fried pastry – decadent but so delicious. Tangy yoghurt, lemon & mint dipping sauce is the perfect partner to samosas. It cuts through the slightly greasy pastry and mellows the spicy filling.

For the filling

3 cups potato and/or kumara, peeled and finely diced

1 tablespoon oil

1 onion, finely diced

2 cloves garlic, crushed

1 thumb ginger, crushed

2 teaspoons ground coriander

2 teaspoons ground cumin

1 teaspoon tumeric

1 teaspoon chilli powder

2 tablespoons garam masala

1 red pepper, chopped

½ cup peas, fresh or frozen

½ cup cashew nuts (optional)

sea salt & freshly ground black pepper

Samosas can be cooked up to a week before serving, and stored in the refrigerator. They can also be frozen for months – thaw to room temperature before using. In both cases, reheat the samosas in an ovenproof dish lined with paper towels.

To make the filling, cook the potatoes and/or kumara in a large saucepan of water until tender. Drain and allow to cool.

In a small saucepan, heat the oil and gently cook the onion, garlic, ginger, coriander, cumin, tumeric and chilli until the onion is softened and the spices have released their flavour.

To the potato/kumara pan, add the onion mixture, garam masala, red pepper, peas and cashew nuts. Season with salt and pepper. Combine well, slightly mashing the potato/kumara.

Making the samosas

5 sheets pre-rolled savoury short pastry

vegetable or light olive oil, for deep frying

yoghurt, lemon & mint dipping sauce (page 92)

To make the samosas, take a sheet of pastry and cut it into a grid of 9 squares. In the middle of each square place a teaspoonful of the samosa filling.

With a small bowl of water to hand, moisten the edges of each pastry square with a wet finger. Fold one corner of each square towards the opposite side; the corners should overlap in the middle, leaving no gap. Press the pastry together enclosing the filling.

Using a small knife trim the samosa to a semi circle shape; you can crimp the edges with a fork if you like.

Pour the oil into a deep-fryer, or a heavy-based saucepan – it need only be about 3cm deep. Heat to about 190°C/370°F (or until a piece of bread browns in 40 seconds). Fry 4–5 samosas at a time for about two minutes each side, until golden and puffed.

As a healthy alternative, bake the samosas, brushed with oil, on a baking tray lined with baking paper, at 180°C/350°F for 10–15 minutes, until golden. They won't have the puffed appearance of fried samosas but will help you feel less guilty.

Place the samosas in an ovenproof dish, lined with paper towels, and keep warm in the oven until ready to serve.

Wraps & balls

Wraps and balls are a popular way of serving finger food all over the world –
in the Mediterranean, South-east Asia, India. They're visually impressive, especially
when piled on platters around a bowl of dipping sauce. Here are my favourites –
guaranteed crowd-pleasers, suitable for any occasion.

**Vietnamese spring rolls
  with dipping sauce** 79

**Suppli with roasted red
  pepper dipping sauce** 80

Prawn balls 82

Pork & sesame balls 83

Sushi 84

**Mandarin pancakes with
  Peking duck** 86

Dolmades 87

Vietnamese spring rolls with dipping sauce

makes 24

Spring rolls are easier to make than you might think – especially Vietnamese spring rolls, which don't require frying. The dipping sauce and spring roll filling are deliciously fragrant and fresh with the combination of mint, ginger and lime. They can be made the day before you wish to serve them.

For the spring rolls

1 handful vermicelli rice noodles

½ cup soybean sprouts, finely chopped

½ cup carrots, grated

2 spring onions, finely chopped

½ cup mint, preferably Vietnamese,
or basil, finely chopped

juice of 1 lime

1 dash fish sauce

1 teaspoon caster sugar

1 tablespoon sweet Thai chilli sauce

24 spring roll wrappers

Pour boiling water into a bowl containing the noodles, and soak for 15 minutes. Drain the noodles thoroughly and chop roughly. Mix together the noodles, bean sprouts, carrots, spring onions and mint. Add the lime juice, fish sauce, sugar and chilli sauce. Mix well.

Pour hot water into a shallow bowl. Take a spring roll wrapper and dunk it in the water; allow it to soften for a minute, then remove and lay on a clean, damp tea towel. Continue with the remaining wrappers, 4–5 at a time. Be careful not to lay them on top of each other – they'll fuse together.

The wrappers are now ready to roll. Place a small handful of the filling in a strip at one end of the wrapper. Roll the wrapper tightly, folding in the sides to enclose the filling. Repeat with the rest of the wrappers and filling. Keep the spring rolls covered in the refrigerator until ready to serve.

Vietnamese dipping sauce

juice of 3 limes

3 tablespoons fish sauce

1 tablespoon caster sugar

1 fresh red chilli, deseeded and finely chopped

1 thumb ginger, grated

Mix together all the ingredients in a bowl.

Suppli with roasted red pepper dipping sauce

makes about 36

In Italy, the risotto ball known as Suppli al Telefono is so named because of the way the melted mozzarella oozes out in strings, just like telephone wires. Suppli can be cooked days before, but when you reheat them make sure the mozzarella is melted in the centre, otherwise the stunning effect is lost.

For the risotto

1½ litres chicken or vegetable stock

100g (3½oz) butter

2 cups risotto rice, such as Arborio

½ cup parmesan, grated

sea salt & freshly ground black pepper

You can use any leftover risotto to make these balls.

To make the rice, place the stock in a saucepan and keep it hot on the stove top. In a large heavy-based saucepan or frying pan, melt half the butter. Add the risotto rice and cook for one minute, until all the grains are coated in the butter and slightly translucent. Add one ladle of hot stock at a time, simmering until the liquid has been absorbed. Stir constantly.

After about 20–25 minutes the rice will be cooked. Test it – the grains should be soft with a hint of bite in the centre. Stir in the remaining butter and parmesan. Season well with salt and pepper. Cover and allow to cool completely.

Roasted red pepper dipping sauce

2 red peppers

1 clove garlic, crushed

½ cup olive oil

sea salt & freshly ground black pepper

Cut the red peppers in half, discard the seeds and membrane, and place under a hot grill, skin-side up, until blistered. Set aside to cool. Once they are cool enough to handle, peel and discard the skins.

In a food processor, blend together the roasted red peppers and garlic. With the motor running, drizzle in the olive oil. Season with salt and pepper.

Making the balls

½ cup pine nuts, toasted

handful of basil, chopped

1 egg

100g (3½oz) mozzarella, preferably buffalo

2 cups dry breadcrumbs

olive oil, for deep frying

Buffalo mozzarella (mozzarella di bufala) is a juicy, delicate cheese made in Italy from the milk of water buffalo. It usually comes in large balls, but is also available in small mouthfuls called bocconcini.

For ease of serving, always provide toothpicks or fancy bamboo cocktail picks. Toothpicks can either be presented in a shot glass, for guests to help themselves, or place a toothpick in each ball.

To toast the pine nuts, place them in a heavy-based frying pan and gently dry-roast. Once they start to brown, keep a close eye on them as they colour quickly.

Mix together the risotto, pine nuts, basil and egg.

Chop the mozzarella into 36 little squares, about ¾cm dice.

Using wet hands, roll the rice mixture into walnut-sized balls. Push a mozzarella square into the middle of each ball and re-roll so the mozzarella is hidden. Make sure the balls are very firmly packed.

Place the breadcrumbs in a large bowl. Roll each ball in the breadcrumbs to coat.

Into a deep-fryer or heavy-based saucepan, pour oil in to about 4cm deep. Heat to 190°C/370°F, or until a piece of bread browns in 40 seconds.

Fry 5–6 suppli at a time for about 3 minutes. Keep turning them to ensure they are evenly browned. Place in an ovenproof dish lined with paper towels, and keep warm in the oven.

Serve the suppli while hot, with a bowl of roasted red pepper dipping sauce and toothpicks.

Prawn balls

This is a very popular finger food that always gets gobbled up in seconds. For me, it has become virtually a catering staple. Serve the prawn balls on a bed of salad greens with a dipping sauce on the side.

500g (18oz) prawn meat, fresh or frozen

2 spring onions, chopped

1 tablespoon flour

sea salt & freshly ground black pepper

oil for deep-frying

Vietnamese dipping sauce (page 79)
or chilli dipping sauce (page 101)

4 limes, quartered, to serve

If using frozen prawns, drain well in a colander and squeeze out any excess liquid.

In a food processor, mix together the prawn meat, spring onions and flour, and season with salt and pepper.

With wet hands, roll the prawn mixture into walnut-sized balls.

Heat the oil in a deep-fryer or heavy-based sauce-pan to 190°C/370°F, or until a piece of bread browns in 40 seconds. The oil should be about 4cm deep.

Fry 5–6 prawn balls at time. Keep turning the prawn balls to ensure they are evenly browned, frying for about three minutes.

Place the balls in an ovenproof dish, lined with paper towels, and keep them warm in the oven.

Serve hot with Vietnamese or chilli dipping sauce, lime wedges and toothpicks.

Pork & sesame balls

Coating these pork balls in sesame seeds, which become nicely browned when fried, makes them very attractive and appetising.

2 slices bread

500g (18oz) pork mince

2 spring onions, chopped

1 thumb ginger, minced

1 clove garlic, crushed

1 tablespoon soy sauce

1 tablespoon oyster sauce

1 tablespoon sweet Thai chilli sauce

½ cup sesame seeds

oil, for deep frying

½ cup plum or sweet Thai chilli sauce, to serve

Pork & sesame balls also make a fantastic meatball sandwich – fill a long roll with hot pork and sesame balls, plum sauce and salad greens.

Preheat oven to 180°C/350°F.

In a food processor, crumb the bread slices. Add the pork mince, spring onions, ginger, garlic, and soy, oyster and sweet Thai chilli sauces, and blend until just combined.

With wet hands, roll the pork mixture into walnut-sized balls. In a large bowl, roll the pork balls in sesame seeds until they are well-covered.

Heat the oil in a deep-fryer or heavy-based sauce-pan to 190°C/370°F, or until a piece of bread browns in 40 seconds. The oil should be about 4cm deep.

Fry 5–6 pork balls at a time. Keep turning the pork balls to ensure they are evenly browned, frying for about three minutes.

Place the pork balls in an ovenproof dish, lined with paper towels. After the last addition of fried pork balls, remove the paper towels and bake the balls in the oven for a further 10 minutes. Open a pork ball and check it is cooked in the middle. Bake a little longer if necessary.

Serve hot with a bowl of plum sauce or sweet Thai chilli sauce and toothpicks.

Sushi

My father has a saying – 'the first pancake is always lumpy'. He is right, and the same is true of sushi. No matter how many times I make sushi, inevitably the first roll is not as neat and tightly rolled as those that follow. Sushi is remarkably easy – and lots of fun!

For the rice

1 cup sushi rice, washed and drained

1½ cups water

4 tablespoons rice vinegar

2 tablespoons caster sugar

1 tablespoon salt

Start by preparing the rice. In a large saucepan, bring the water to the boil, add the rice and simmer, covered, for 15 minutes. Let stand, covered, for 10 minutes. The water should have been absorbed, leaving the rice rather sticky.

Stir in the vinegar, sugar and salt. Cover and allow to cool.

....

Sushi fillings

There are many possible choices for sushi fillings, so I suggest offering a selection. When preparing your fillings, remember that they have to roll – so thin strips and small portions of ingredients are best.

smoked salmon and avocado slices

a vegetable medley of carrot and cucumber sticks, pepper, spring onion and avocado slices

tinned tuna (drained) mixed with a little wasabi mayonnaise (page 63), and cucumber sticks

shredded poached chicken mixed with a little teriyaki sauce, and red pepper slices

omelette, made with 1 egg and a dash of soy sauce, halved and chopped spring onions, and red pepper slices

To assemble and serve

4 sheets nori

½ cup soy sauce, preferably Japanese

¼ cup pickled ginger

2 teaspoons wasabi

You can also roll up sushi rice on its own, then top with something interesting such as butterflied prawn tails, or slices of smoked salmon with black (or toasted) sesame seeds, or fish roe.

Now you're ready to roll.

The secret to sushi is not to overfill. Little sushi rounds that are one mouthful are best because they are easiest to eat.

Lay a sheet of nori, shiny-side down, on a sushi mat or clean tea towel. Using wet hands, press on a thin layer of rice (so it just covers up the nori), leaving 5cm uncovered at the far edge.

At the edge closest to you, place your chosen filling in a strip across the sushi rice – the filling strip should be about 2–3cm wide. Lightly dampen the tail end (uncovered edge) with water.

With help from the sushi mat or tea towel, tightly roll the sushi away from you: you're beginning at the filling end, and finishing with the damp end, which seals the roll closed.

Wrap each roll tightly in plastic wrap. Refrigerate for at least 30 minutes, and up to one day, before serving.

To serve, remove the roll from the plastic wrap. With a sharp knife, slice it into 2cm slices. Arrange the sushi slices on a platter, and present with traditional accompaniments: a small bowl of soy sauce, another of pickled ginger, and a tiny saucer of wasabi.

Mandarin pancakes with Peking duck

makes 24–30

Peking duck can be bought from your local Chinese restaurant or takeaway, but you can of course use your own home-made roast duck or chicken. The pancakes can be made ahead of time; just store them covered in the refrigerator, and reheat gently in the oven or microwave before serving.

Mandarin pancakes

2½ cups plain flour

2 teaspoons caster sugar

1 cup boiling water

1 tablespoon sesame oil

oil for frying

To make the pancakes, combine the flour and sugar and gradually pour in the boiling water, stirring with a wooden spoon until mixed. Leave until lukewarm, then knead on a lightly floured surface until smooth. Cover and set aside for 30 minutes.

Take a golf ball-sized piece of dough. Divide in two. Roll each piece into a 5cm diameter circle. Brush one circle with sesame oil, and place the other circle on top. Re-roll to make a thin double pancake about 10cm in diameter. Repeat with the rest of the dough.

Heat a frying pan brushed with oil. Cook the pancakes one at a time. When bubbles appear on the surface, turn over and cook the other side. Transfer the pancakes to a plate. When they are cool enough to handle, peel each apart into its 2 halves.

Peking duck

1 Peking duck

1 small cucumber

2 spring onions

½ cup hoisin sauce or plum sauce

fresh chives, full length

Hoisin sauce is a spicy condiment available in Asian food shops and supermarkets.

Carve the duck into thin slices, attempting to leave some skin on each slice. Deseed the cucumber and cut into matchsticks. Thinly slice the spring onions on the diagonal. Quickly blanch the chives in boiling water and run under cold water.

Spread a little hoisin or plum sauce on each pancake, browned side down. Add a little of the duck, cucumber and spring onions. Roll up each pancake and tie firmly with a chive, trimming if too long.

Dolmades

Dolmades are a healthy and tasty Greek delicacy, which can be prepared up to two weeks in advance of your party. Just store them covered in the refrigerator. They also need very little attention on the day.

1 onion, finely chopped

3 tablespoons olive oil

½ cup long-grain rice

1 cup water

¼ cup pine nuts, toasted (page 30)

¼ cup currants or raisins

¼ cup parsley, chopped

sea salt & freshly ground black pepper

24 preserved vine leaves

1 cup water

juice of 1 lemon

Use fresh vine leaves if you are lucky enough to have them handy. Choose nice unblemished leaves. Blanch by dunking each in boiling water for 1 minute, and then plunging into cold water. Trim off the stems.

Sauté the onion in olive oil in a frying pan. Add the rice and cook until the grains have absorbed some of the oil and become a little translucent. Add 1 cup of water, pine nuts, currants, parsley, salt and pepper. Cover with a lid and cook gently for 10–12 minutes, until the rice is tender and the liquid has been absorbed. Allow to cool.

Rinse the vine leaves, pat dry, and spread smooth-side down on a bench. Trim the vine leaves of any stems that may pierce the leaf when rolled up.

Divide the rice filling between the vine leaves. Roll up each leaf tightly, tucking in the ends as you go. Make sure you don't overfill the dolmades – no filling should ooze out.

In a large pan, tightly pack the dolmades in a single layer. Pour over 1 cup of water and squeeze on the lemon juice. Place a large heatproof plate on top and cover with a lid. Bring to the boil and gently simmer for 45 minutes, or until tender. Check a few times to make sure the water hasn't completely evaporated. Allow the dolmades to cool in the pan with the lid on.

Serve on their own, or with yoghurt, lemon & mint sauce (page 92).

Skewers

Food on sticks appears in many cultures and has many names – among them, skewers, kebabs and satays. They are a particularly good food choice for outdoor parties, as they can be cooked on the barbecue and served immediately. The cook remains part of the party, not stuck in the kitchen.

Lime & ginger chicken skewers

makes 24

These delicious skewers will be appreciated by low-carbohydrate dieters and are also a tasty addition to a barbecue spread. Chicken tenderloins are great for skewers: you are assured of a moist result and no chopping is required – simply thread them, like a ribbon, on to each skewer.

24 bamboo skewers

24 chicken tenderloins, or skinless chicken breast cut into strips or chunks

2 limes, coarsely grated zest and squeezed juice

1 thumb ginger, crushed

¼ cup oil

sea salt & freshly ground black pepper

satay dip (page 17)

For another simple marinade for chicken or beef skewers, combine 1 crushed garlic clove, 1 tablespoon honey, 2 tablespoons peanut oil and ¼ cup light soy sauce. This also goes well with satay dip.

Soak the bamboo skewers in water for at least 30 minutes to prevent them burning.

In a bowl, mix together the chicken, lime zest and juice, ginger, oil, salt and pepper. Cover and marinate in the refrigerator for at least 30 minutes, preferably overnight.

Thread the chicken on to the bamboo skewers, one chicken tenderloin per skewer.

Either cook the skewers on an oiled griddle or barbecue, or under a hot grill in the oven – on a greased rack over a roasting dish. Turn on to all sides, until brown and cooked through. (Check by breaking one in half.)

Serve immediately with satay dip.

Smoked paprika & yoghurt chicken skewers

makes 24

The combination of yoghurt and smoked paprika is scrummy – it has an almost Tandoori flavour – and the yoghurt makes for extra-succulent chicken.

24 bamboo skewers

24 chicken tenderloins, or 3 skinless chicken breasts cut into strips or chunks

1 tablespoon smoked paprika, hot or sweet according to taste

1 cup natural yoghurt

juice of 1 lemon

sea salt & freshly ground black pepper

oil, for grilling

yoghurt, lemon & mint dipping sauce (below) or guacamole (page 20)

Smoked paprika is ground smoked red peppers – the best comes from Spain. It's worth spending money to get an authentic high-quality product. It comes in hot or sweet varieties – the hot one is very hot.

Soak the bamboo skewers in water at least 30 minutes to prevent them from burning.

In a bowl, mix together the chicken, smoked paprika, yoghurt and lemon juice and season with salt and pepper. Cover and marinate in the refrigerator for at least 30 minutes, preferably overnight.

Thread the chicken on to the bamboo skewers, shaking off any excess marinade.

The skewers can either be cooked on an oiled griddle or barbecue, or under a hot grill in the oven – on a greased rack over a roasting dish. Turn on all sides until brown and cooked through. (Break one in half to check that it is cooked.)

Serve with yoghurt, lemon & mint dipping sauce or guacamole.

....

Yoghurt, lemon & mint dipping sauce

1 cup natural yoghurt

juice of 1 lemon

½ cup mint, finely chopped

sea salt & freshly ground black pepper

Combine the yoghurt, lemon juice, mint, salt and pepper in a bowl, or pulse together in a food processor or blender. Let sit at least 30 minutes before serving to let the flavours develop.

Prawn & snow pea skewers

Delicious, healthy and simple.

24 bamboo skewers
24 fresh uncooked prawns
olive oil
sea salt & freshly ground black pepper
juice of 1 lemon
24 snow peas

The first step is to prepare the prawns if they are in their shells. Pull the head away from the tail section and discard. Remove the shell and the tail. Fold the prawn down the middle, and with a toothpick remove the intestinal thread, along the outer curve.

The prawns now need to be steamed, either in a Chinese bamboo steamer or an ordinary saucepan steamer. First, brush them with oil, then place in the steamer and season with salt and pepper. Squeeze over lemon juice, and steam with the lid on for about 4 minutes, until the prawns are opaque. Remove and set aside.

Blanch the snow peas – dunk in boiling water for 1 minute, then refresh under running cold water.

To make a skewer, thread one end of a snow pea then both ends of a prawn. Finally bend the snow pea over the prawn and thread on the other end.

Serve warm or at room temperature.

Bacon & prune skewers

Classic 'devils on horseback' made modern. Make sure you let the skewers cool a little before serving – the natural sugars in the prunes can get very hot.

24 bamboo skewers

48 pitted prunes

12 rashers bacon, cut in half

olive oil

sea salt & freshly ground black pepper

Try thinly smearing cream cheese on to the prunes before grilling – it will caramelise deliciously.

Soak the bamboo skewers in water for at least 30 minutes.

Thread 2 prunes and a piece of bacon on to each skewer: ribbon-weave and wrap the prunes in the bacon as you skewer them.

The skewers can be cooked either on an oiled griddle or barbecue, or under a hot grill in the oven – on a greased rack over a roasting dish. Turn on to all sides until the bacon is crisp and browned.

Serve immediately.

Asparagus & prosciutto skewers

makes 24

No bamboo skewers here – the asparagus spear is the skewer! Choose similarly sized spears so they cook evenly. This is a real spring treat.

24 asparagus spears

24 strips prosciutto

1 tablespoon balsamic vinegar

2 tablespoons olive oil

sea salt & freshly ground black pepper

Snap the woody end off each asparagus spear, and then wash the spear thoroughly to remove any nasty grit.

Wrap in a strip of prosciutto twisting up the length of the asparagus spear.

Drizzle the wrapped asparagus with balsamic vinegar and olive oil, and season with salt and pepper.

Grill or fry until crisp and golden, turning on to all sides.

Serve warm.

....

Asparagus spears are also delicious served simply with orange mayonnaise. Grill or fry the spears with balsamic vinegar, olive oil, salt and pepper.

To make the orange mayonnaise, make mayonnaise (page 50), replacing the lemon juice with orange juice and adding one tablespoon of finely grated orange zest.

Fritters

Fritters and savoury cakes are simple to make, but it is important to have a reliable non-stick pan to work with. All these can also be served for lunches or light suppers: make about six individual fritters or cakes from each recipe, and serve with a green salad.

Corn fritters with salsa

If you have canned corn in the pantry you can easily whip up these corn fritters whenever you like. Heating the fritters in the oven after frying ensures that all the flour is cooked through – no horrible glugginess.

1¾ cups (200g/7oz) plain flour, sifted

2 teaspoons baking powder

1 cup corn kernels

1 cup creamed corn

½ cup milk

2 eggs, beaten

handful chives, half finely chopped, half for decoration

sea salt & freshly ground black pepper

vegetable oil, for frying

salsa (page 21) or crème fraîche dip (page 102)

An alternative topping for these corn fritters is cream cheese spread (page 49) and smoked salmon. Sprinkle with finely chopped chives.

Preheat the oven to 160°C/325°F.

Mix together the flour and baking powder in a bowl. Make a well in the centre and add the corn kernels and creamed corn, milk, eggs and chopped chives. Mix well and let rest for 30 minutes.

Heat the oil in a non-stick frying pan for shallow frying. Dollop teaspoonfuls of the corn mixture into the frying pan; do about 5 or 6 at a time. Using a pair of teaspoons, shape the corn mixture into rounds and flatten a little. Fry until golden brown on both sides.

Place the fritters on a paper towel-lined baking tray and keep warm in the oven.

To serve, top each fritter with a teaspoonful of salsa or crème fraîche dip and a criss-cross of chives. Serve warm.

Thai fish cakes with chilli dipping sauce

makes about 24

Serve these Thai fish cakes with flair – by placing each fish cake in the pincers of takeaway chopsticks. Just open the chopstick ends a little and nudge a fish cake into the gap, being careful not to snap the chopsticks in half.

500g (18oz) firm white fish fillets, such as butterfish

3 tablespoons cornflour

1 tablespoon fish sauce

1 egg

½ cup fresh coriander

1 tablespoon ready-made red curry paste

2 spring onions, finely chopped

vegetable oil, for frying

Add ½ cup of toasted desiccated coconut to the fish cake mixture, when adding the spring onions, for a crunchier texture.

Blend the fish in a food processor until smooth. Add the cornflour, fish sauce, egg, coriander and red curry paste. Process until combined.

Transfer the mixture into a bowl and stir in the spring onions.

Using wet hands, mold into flattish patties, about 4cm in diameter.

Heat a generous amount of oil in a frying pan. Cook 6 fish cakes at a time until browned on both sides. Slip them into a paper towel-lined roasting pan, keeping warm in a moderate oven.

Serve warm with chilli dipping sauce.

Chilli dipping sauce

½ cup sugar

½ cup water

½ cup white wine vinegar

1 tablespoon fish sauce

1 red chilli, deseeded & finely chopped

¼ small cucumber, deseeded & chopped

1 tablespoon peanuts, roasted & chopped
(optional)

You can prepare these fish cakes a few hours
ahead of time. Simply warm them in the oven
before serving. They won't be as good as freshly
cooked fish cakes: they'll be just a little stodgier.
But, if you don't want your kitchen, or yourself
for that matter, smelling of hot oil and fish, it's
a trade-off worth making.

In a small pan, combine the sugar, water, vinegar
and fish sauce. Bring to the boil and simmer for
five minutes until it thickens a little. Remove from
heat.

When the liquid is cool, add the red chilli, cucumber
and peanuts (optional).

Spanish fish cakes with crème fraîche dip

makes about 24

Hot-smoked salmon is perfect for this recipe, as the salmon flakes are easily combined with the potato mash.

4–5 floury potatoes, quartered

200g (7oz) hot-smoked salmon, flaked

2 spring onions, finely chopped

½ cup parsley, chopped

½ cup coriander, chopped

3 eggs, beaten

sea salt & freshly ground black pepper

milk

1 cup plain flour

1½ cups dry breadcrumbs

olive oil for frying

Preheat the oven to 180°C/350°F.

Cook the potatoes in boiling salted water until soft, about 15 minutes. Drain and then return them to the hot pan to dry.

Mash the potatoes. Stir in the fish, spring onions, herbs and one-third of the beaten egg. Season with salt and pepper and mix well to form a firm mash, adding a little milk if necessary. Roll into golf-sized balls. Flatten and shape into cakes.

Place the remaining beaten egg, flour and bread-crumbs into separate bowls. Roll each fish cake in flour, then beaten egg, and finally breadcrumbs.

In a non-stick frying pan, heat oil for shallow frying. Fry 5–6 cakes at a time until golden brown, about two minutes on each side. Add extra oil as necessary. Place the fish cakes in an ovenproof dish, lined with paper towels, and keep warm in the oven.

Serve warm with crème fraîche dip.

Crème fraîche dip

1 cup crème fraîche

finely grated zest & juice of 1 lime or lemon

¼ cup white wine

sea salt & pepper, preferably white

Mix together all the ingredients in a bowl.

Whitebait fritters

Take advantage of the whitebait season by making these delicately flavoured fritters. Serve with slices of fresh white bread and butter for a more substantial meal.

500g (18oz) whitebait

4 eggs, separated

4 tablespoons flour

½ teaspoon baking soda

sea salt & freshly ground black pepper

finely grated zest of 1 lemon

4 tablespoons milk

oil & butter for frying

lemon wedges, to serve

Combine the whitebait, egg yolks, flour, baking powder, lemon zest and seasoning in a bowl. In another bowl, whisk the egg whites until stiff. Fold the egg whites into the whitebait mixture. Use the mixture immediately.

In a frying pan, heat 1 teaspoon each of oil and butter (for colour) until they start to sizzle. Add spoonfuls of the whitebait mixture – about 4–5 at a time, frying for 1–2 minutes on each side, or until golden brown. Add more butter and oil as necessary.

Keep the fritters warm on a plate in the oven until ready to serve.

Serve warm with lemon wedges.

Little fish

I find that seafood, particularly shellfish, is always a huge success at parties. If any of your guests are from overseas, these dishes provide a wonderful opportunity to showcase some of New Zealand's fantastic treats from the ocean. Most seafood needs little treatment – the simpler and fresher the better.

Beer-battered fish bites with garlic & lemon mayonnaise

Beer batter makes for a great talking point, and a superb crispy coating for fish.

500g (18oz) firm white fish, such as butterfish

1 cup plain flour, sifted

2 pinches salt

2 tablespoons olive oil

finely grated zest & juice of 1 lemon

⅔ cup beer, preferably lager, or soda water

1 egg white

vegetable oil, for frying

As an alternative to fish, try using freshly shucked oysters or marinated mussels, with garlic and lemon mayonnaise as a dip.

Cut the fish into bite-sized pieces. In a bowl, mix together the sifted flour and salt, making a well in the middle. Add the olive oil and gradually add the beer, stirring with a wooden spoon until the batter is completely smooth. Allow to rest for at least half an hour, preferably 2 hours.

When ready to fry, whisk the egg white and gently fold into the batter. Heat the oil in a deep-fryer or heavy-based saucepan to 190°C/370°F, or until a piece of bread browns in 40 seconds. The oil should be about 4cm deep.

Dip the fish, piece by piece, into the batter. Fry 4–5 pieces at a time until golden brown. Place on a paper towel-lined ovenproof dish and keep warm in a moderate oven.

Serve with garlic & lemon mayonnaise.

Garlic & lemon mayonnaise

1 egg

1 pinch sugar

1 pinch salt

1 pinch pepper, preferably white

finely grated zest & juice of 1 lemon

1 clove garlic, crushed

1 cup vegetable oil

In a food processor, blend together all ingredients, except two-thirds of the oil. When this mixture has emulsified, slowly drizzle in the remaining oil with the motor running. Add more seasoning if required.

Oysters with dipping sauce

Personally, I'm not particularly oyster savvy. My advice would be to serve oysters on the shell only if you, or someone attending your party, is an experienced oyster shucker – it is not recommended for first-timers as you are likely to have an accident. However, for the adventurous, here's how to do it. You can, of course, do what I do: buy already shucked oysters, and serve in a bowl with toothpicks.

24 oysters

3 handfuls crushed ice

6 lemons, quartered

Scrub the oyster shells with a stiff brush.

Place the oyster on a firm surface with the hinged end towards you and flattest side upwards. Protect the hand you will use to hold the oyster in an oven glove or by wrapping in a tea towel.

Insert a very sharp, smallish knife into the oyster where the shell is hinged. Release the muscle holding the oyster to the shell by employing a levering action with the knife, and a fair bit of elbow grease. Twist off the top shell and discard.

Ensure the oyster is completely released from the shell by running the knife under and around the oyster.

To make a bed of ice for the oysters, take a bag of ice cubes and bash with a heavy mallet or rolling pin. Take a platter with a lip and pour crushed ice on to it. Place the half-shelled oysters on top. Scatter the lemon quarters around the oysters.

Serve with one or both of the dipping sauces opposite.

Classic French dipping sauce

½ cup red wine vinegar

1–2 tablespoons sugar

½ cup parsley, chopped

1 shallot, finely chopped

Combine all ingredients in a bowl, adjusting the sugar to taste.

. . . .

Chilli & lime dipping sauce

½ cup rice wine vinegar

2–4 teaspoons sugar

½ cup coriander, chopped

½ fresh red chilli, finely chopped

thin strips of zest and squeezed juice of 1 lime

dash of fish sauce

Combine all ingredients in a bowl, adjusting the sugar to taste.

Grilled mussels

makes 24

Mussels are the perfect party shellfish because they're easy to prepare, difficult to ruin and very economical. See how appealing they are as they come out from under the grill with their hot, crunchy breadcrumb topping!

24 unopened fresh mussels

1 cup white wine or water, approximately

choice of toppings, below

½ cup butter, melted

sea salt & freshly ground black pepper

Preheat the oven grill to high.

Place the mussels in a deep, wide-lidded saucepan or wok. Pour in enough wine (or water) to cover the bottom of the pan by about 1cm. Put the lid on and turn the heat on full. Cook for 5 minutes. Remove all the opened mussels, and cook the remaining unopened mussels for another minute or two. Those that remain unopened should now be discarded. Allow the cooked mussels to cool.

Pull off and discard the mussel beard and top half of the shell. Using a knife, ensure that the mussel is dislodged from the shell.

Arrange the half-shelled mussels, tightly packed, in an ovenproof dish. Sprinkle your chosen bread-crumb topping on each mussel. Spoon over the melted butter and season with salt and pepper.

Grill for 2–3 minutes until golden brown. Serve immediately.

Mussel toppings

In a food processor, blend together either:

½ cup parmesan, ½ cup parsley, two slices of fresh bread & a clove of garlic, or

½ cup pinenuts, ½ cup fresh dill, two slices of fresh bread & grated zest of 1 lemon

Scallops on Asian coleslaw

makes 12

A party-food cookbook is not complete without a dish served in Asian soup spoons – they're all the rage. However, if you don't have them, use cleaned scallop shells or attractive dessertspoons instead.

12 Asian soup spoons

12 queen scallops off the shell, with or without coral

3 tablespoons vegetable oil

juice of 1 lime

1 teaspoon brown sugar

1 dash fish sauce

1 tablespoon sweet Thai chilli sauce

½ cup soy bean sprouts, finely chopped

1 spring onion, finely chopped

2cm piece cucumber, deseeded & finely diced

4 snow peas (optional), finely sliced

½ cup coriander or mint, finely chopped, plus extra leaves for presentation

If using frozen scallops, thaw them in the refrigerator on a wad of paper towels, the day you wish to use them. If using fresh scallops, purchase them the day before or the day of your party.

To make the dressing, mix together the vegetable oil, lime juice, brown sugar, fish sauce and chilli sauce.

For the coleslaw, mix together the finely chopped bean sprouts, spring onions, cucumber and snow peas, together with the coriander or mint.

Cook the scallops just before you're ready to serve them. Pour a tablespoon or so of vegetable oil into a heavy-based frying pan. On a moderately high temperature, heat the oil for about a minute. Add the scallops and sear for 2 minutes, then turn them over and sear for another minute. Don't fuss with the scallops; just let them cook undisturbed.

In each Asian soup spoon, place a small mound of coleslaw. Place a seared scallop on top and drizzle over a teaspoonful of dressing. Place a small mint or coriander leaf on top.

Serve immediately.

Christmas parties

The Christmas season is the busiest time of year for entertaining – and just about everything else! These recipes are designed to help you achieve stunning results with minimal fuss. I believe in having fun with food. I hope you'll love the creative use of Christmas colours and be inspired to dream up more ideas of your own.

These recipes are perfect for serving both at pre-Christmas parties, and on Christmas Day, when visitors are having their main meal elsewhere and want only a light snack.

You can of course mix and match them with recipes from other sections. Try:

Asparagus & prosciutto skewers (page 95) – an easy and healthy seasonal option

Chilli orange pork pies (page 70) – my family's Christmas favourite

Panini fingers (page 45) filled with **roast turkey** (page 116) and cranberry sauce

Pissaladière (page 56) and **spinach cheesy tarts** (page 58) arranged into a red and green chequerboard

Pizzetta (page 46) topped with summer vegetables

Salmon & wasabi cucumber cups (page 62)

Summer dips – guacamole (page 20) & **salsa** (page 21)

Summer fruit tarts (page 126), topped with red berries and dusted with sieved icing sugar

Roast turkey, cranberry & stuffing squares

makes 40

Combined with new potatoes with minted pea purée (see following page), the result is a mini Christmas roast meal in a couple of mouthfuls.

Roast turkey

1 turkey breast, with skin on

2 tablespoons oil

sea salt & freshly ground black pepper

Preheat the oven to 180°C/350°F.

Rub the turkey breast in oil, season with salt and pepper, and wrap in aluminium foil. Place on a rack in a shallow roasting pan and roast for 2 hours. Open the foil and test the breast is cooked by piercing through the middle – the juices should run clear. Cook a further 30 minutes if it still looks a little pink.

Cool the cooked turkey breast fully while still in the foil – this will keep it moist.

Sage & onion stuffing

2 tablespoons butter or oil

1 small onion, finely diced

4 slices white or multigrain bread, ripped into small pieces

1 egg

1 tablespoon fresh or dried sage, finely chopped

sea salt & freshly ground black pepper

Preheat the oven to 180°C/350°F.

Sauté the onions in half the butter or oil until soft. Remove from heat and add the bread, egg and sage, and season with salt and pepper. Mix well. Add more bread if the mixture is a bit wet.

Grease a 30cm piece of aluminium foil with remaining butter or oil. Place the stuffing in the middle of the foil and fashion into a fat sausage. Wrap and twist the foil like a large wrapped sweetie.

Bake for 30 minutes. Allow to cool.

Making the squares

roast turkey

sage & onion stuffing

10 slices white or multigrain bread, sandwich sliced

butter, or similar spread

2–3 tablespoons of cranberry sauce

40 toothpicks

Give your toothpicks Christmas flair by gluing a festive sequin, such as a silver star, on to the end of each.

Thinly slice the turkey breast against the grain. With a bread knife, thinly slice the stuffing. Don't worry if it crumbles a little.

Lay out 5 slices of bread and butter them lightly. Top with slices of turkey, then slices of stuffing. On the remaining 5 bread slices, spread a little cranberry sauce, and pop them on top of the filled bottoms.

With a bread knife, trim off the crusts and cut into 4 squares. Secure each square with a toothpick.

These are best made the day you wish to eat them – no one likes a soggy sammy.

These sandwiches can also be served toasted. Before cutting into squares, simply toast in a lightly greased sandwich press, or very quickly under an oven grill.

New potatoes with minted pea purée

This recipe is a celebration of summer vegetables. A small shell of new potato filled with vibrant, sweet, green pea purée, topped with a criss-cross of roasted red pepper – delicious and visually dramatic. Serve straight from the oven or at room temperature.

New potatoes

24 small new potatoes, as evenly sized as possible

3 tablespoons olive oil

sea salt & freshly ground black pepper

Preheat the oven to 200°C/390°F.

Cut a thin slice off one side of each potato to create a flat base. Rub the potatoes with olive oil and season with salt and pepper, and roast in a baking paper-lined roasting pan for about 20 minutes, until tender. Allow to cool.

Minted pea purée

1 cup fresh or frozen peas

1 sprig fresh mint

2 tablespoons crème fraîche

sea salt & freshly ground black pepper

Place the peas and mint in a saucepan of water and bring to the boil. Simmer for a few minutes until tender. Drain the peas, reserving 2 tablespoons of the cooking water. Discard the mint. Allow to cool.

In a food processor, blend the peas, adding the reserved cooking water until the consistency reaches a rough paste. Transfer to a bowl and mix in the crème fraîche, seasoning with salt and pepper to taste.

To assemble

1 roasted red pepper (page 30), cut into 2cm strips

Using a small sharp knife and a teaspoon, make a hollow in the top of each potato. Fill with minted pea purée and top with a criss-cross of roasted red pepper.

Bake the filled potatoes at 180°C/350°F for 10–15 minutes until heated through.

Angels on horseback

This recipe uses water chestnuts, instead of the traditional oysters. Canned water chestnuts are readily available in supermarkets.

24 toothpicks
24 water chestnuts
12 rashers bacon, cut in half
1 teaspoon honey
1 tablespoon soy sauce
1 tablespoon oil

To make traditional angels on horseback, simply replace the water chestnuts with shucked and cleaned oysters or scallops.

Soak the toothpicks in water for at least 30 minutes.

Wrap each water chestnut in a rasher of bacon and secure with a toothpick.

Mix together the honey, soy sauce and oil, and brush on to the bacon-wrapped chestnuts.

Bake on a baking paper-lined tray at 200°C/390°F for about 20 minutes, until the bacon is crisp and browned.

Serve immediately.

Festive fruit compote tarts

These are delicious with a tipple or two of brandy at the end of a night's partying. Or share them with your workmates as a lighter alternative to ready-made traditional Christmas mince pies.

½ cup dried cranberries

½ cup raisins

½ cup glacé cherries, roughly chopped

½ cup dried apricots, roughly chopped

zest and juice of 1 orange

1 cup sugar

½ cup water

½ cup brandy

1 cinnamon stick

½ cup flaked almonds

1 quantity sweet tart cases (page 126)

The fruit in the recipe can be replaced with any alternatives – try dried tropical fruits such as mango, papaya and pineapple.

Place all the fruit, orange zest and juice, sugar, water, brandy and cinnamon stick in a saucepan and bring to the boil. Simmer for 5 minutes. Allow to cool completely. Discard the cinnamon stick and place the fruit in a sieve, catching all the lovely fruity liquid in a separate saucepan. Set the stewed fruit aside.

Bring the fruity liquid to the boil and simmer until it is reduced to a syrupy consistency, then allow to cool.

In an oven preheated to 200°C/390°F, toast the flaked almonds until golden.

To serve, spoon the stewed fruit into the prepared tart cases. Spoon over a little fruit syrup, and top with a sprinkle of the almond flakes.

These are best served the same day, although the filling and the tart cases will keep, separately, for a couple of weeks.

Chocolate-dipped cherries

Cherries are highly evocative of Christmas. Our family always has a big bowl on hand on Christmas Day, and we try to tie the stems into knots with our tongues. The stems are, of course, also useful for holding the cherries for dipping.

500g (18oz) chocolate, best quality you can afford

2 tablespoons cherry liqueur, Amaretto or brandy

24 fresh cherries, stems on

This recipe also works well for strawberries.

Wash and dry the cherries thoroughly.

Smash the chocolate while it is still in its wrapper. Put the broken chocolate and liquor into the top of a double boiler (or a heat-resistant bowl placed over a saucepan of gently simmering water, making sure the water does not touch the bottom of the bowl). Gently heat the mixture, stirring occasionally, until melted. Remove from the heat.

Holding the cherries by the stem, dip them one by one into the melted chocolate. Place on baking paper or plastic wrap until the chocolate hardens.

Amaretto rose

The perfect Christmas cocktail would have to include Amaretto, an almond-flavoured liqueur reminiscent of marzipan and other Christmas sweets. Very refreshing for hot, sunny Christmas parties – fingers crossed.

3 shots Amaretto

1 shot lime juice

ice

soda water, to top up

1 red glacé cherry

1 green glacé cherry

1 toothpick

Pour Amaretto and lime juice over ice in a tall glass, and top up with soda water. Place a red and green glacé cherry on a toothpick and balance on the top of the glass for decoration.

Sweets

Serving something small and sweet often makes for a delightful end to a party, especially when it is accompanied by aromatic freshly-ground coffee, a selection of special fragrant teas and/or a dessert wine. When I'm catering for an event, I always like to include sweets that are petite and attractive.

Fortune cookies

Fortune cookies are fun. You can put any message inside – fortunes, personal notes, famous quotes, jokes or publicity gimmicks. One crazy night I made fortune cookies with dares in them – that really made things interesting!

3 egg whites
½ cup icing sugar, sifted
50g (2oz) butter, melted
½ cup plain flour, sifted
30 fortunes, on small strips of paper

Preheat the oven to 180°C/350°F.

Line a baking tray with baking paper, and draw on 3 circles, 8cm in diameter.

In a clean bowl, whisk the egg whites until just frothy. Add the icing sugar and melted butter, mixing until smooth. Fold in the flour, gently mixing until smooth. Let stand for 15 minutes.

Using a flat-bladed knife, spread 1½ teaspoons of mixture on to each drawn circle. Bake for 5 minutes until slightly browned.

Now you need to work quickly – these three cookies will cool quickly and become too crisp to fold.

Remove each cookie from the tray with a flat-bladed knife. Place a paper message in the centre. Fold the cookie in half to form a semi-circle, then fold it over the edge of a glass to form the familiar fortune-cookie shape – a bit like a banana. Leave to cool on a wire rack.

Repeat with the rest of the cookie batter.

Summer fruit or citrus tarts

For this recipe, it's well worth the effort making the pastry cases from scratch. This pastry, based on my family's famous neenish tart recipe, gives a beautiful biscuity base – just as good as the filling.

Sweet tart cases

115g (4oz) butter

115g (4oz) sugar

1 small egg

225g (8oz) flour, plus extra for rolling

1 teaspoon baking powder

1 pinch salt

Cream the butter and sugar in a food processor until pale. Add the egg and mix well. Add the flour, baking powder and salt and mix on a low speed until the pastry comes together in a ball.

Wrap the pastry ball in plastic wrap and rest in the refrigerator for 30 minutes.

Preheat the oven to 180°C/350°F.

Divide the pastry dough in two. Roll each half out on a well-floured bench, remembering to flour the top of the pastry to prevent the rolling pin from sticking. Roll the pastry out to about 5mm thick.

Cut out rounds of pastry using pastry cutters, or an upturned drinking glass and sharp knife, to fit the mini-muffin tins. Push the pastry rounds into the tins and prick the base a few times with a fork, to reduce puffing.

Bake the pastry cases in the oven for 10–15 minutes until very slightly browned. Allow the cases to cool in the muffin tins until hard enough to remove without altering the shape. Leave to fully cool on a wire rack.

Store the cases in an airtight container in a cool place, but not the refrigerator. They will last a couple of weeks.

The tart cases can be filled with either of these equally tantalising fillings – cheesecake-style summer fruit or tangy citrus, with your choice of lemon, lime or orange. The summer fruit tart needs to be eaten straight after filling, while the citrus tart can be made up to a week in advance.

Summer fruit filling

½ cup mascarpone

⅓ cup fresh cream, lightly whipped

4 tablespoons icing sugar, sifted

1 teaspoon vanilla extract or essence

summer fruits – a selection of berries, tropical or stone fruits

½ cup apricot jam or marmalade

Mix together the mascarpone, cream, icing sugar and vanilla. Prepare fruit by hulling, stoning, and slicing thinly into delicate pieces. Fill the tart cases with the filling and top with the fruit.

Heat the jam or marmalade and strain through a sieve. While hot, brush on top of the fruit to give a pretty gloss.

Serve immediately.

Citrus filling

8 lemon, lime or orange slices, about 3mm wide

½ cup water

1 cup sugar

8 tablespoons sweetened condensed milk

150g (5oz) butter, softened

4 tablespoons icing sugar, sifted

finely grated zest & juice of 1 lemon, lime or half an orange

Place the citrus slices, water and sugar in a small saucepan. Bring to the boil and simmer until transparent. Remove fruit and cool on a wire rack.

Combine the condensed milk, butter, icing sugar, citrus zest and juice in a bowl. Spoon this mixture into the tart cases, working quickly, as the filling will soon set. Fill almost to the top.

Cut each dried citrus slice into 6 segments, and place a segment on each tart.

The filled citrus tarts will last up to a week. Keep in single layers in airtight containers in a cool place, but not the refrigerator.

Berry ripple

makes 6–12 depending on glass size

Stripes of meringue cream and berries look stunning served in individual glasses. Use shot, aperitif or wine glasses, or champagne flutes. Home-made meringues are better than ready-made as they have a much better texture.

250g strawberries and/or raspberries

½ cup caster sugar

1 tablespoon lemon or orange juice

⅔ cup fresh cream, lightly whipped

1 teaspoon vanilla extract or essence

4 small meringues, ready-made, or home-made, as below

basil or mint leaves, for decoration

Instead of whipped cream, try using mascarpone or natural Greek-style yoghurt.

In a food processor or blender, combine half the berries with the sugar and lemon or orange juice. Pass this berry coulis through a sieve to remove any seeds. Slice or halve the remaining berries.

Crumble the meringue and combine with the cream and vanilla.

Layer meringue cream, berry coulis and berries in each glass, starting and ending with meringue cream.

Decorate with basil or mint leaves and serve with a teaspoon.

. . . .

Meringues

4 egg whites

225g (8oz) caster sugar

Preheat the oven to 140°C/275°F.

In a clean bowl, whisk the egg whites, adding the sugar little by little, until firm peaks are formed.

On a baking tray lined with baking paper, divide the mixture into 4 rounds.

Bake for 10 minutes, then turn off the heat. Allow to completely cool in the oven, with the door closed. This should take about 1½–2 hours. Your meringues should ideally remain white in colour, and be dry and crisp right through.

Chocolate brownies

These soft brownies are perfect as a simple sweet treat to accompany coffee at the end of the night. They can be made well in advance, and will store very well wrapped in tin foil.

250g (9oz) chocolate

250g (9oz) butter

2 cups sugar

2 teaspoons vanilla extract or essence

4 eggs

1½ cups plain white flour, sifted

½ cup cocoa, sifted

¼ cup icing sugar, sifted, for presentation

For a colourful presentation, sprinkle the brownies with the petals and heads of edible flowers – pansies, nasturtiums, dandelions, carnations, violets or roses.

Preheat the oven to 180°C/350°F.

Smash the chocolate while still in its wrapper, and transfer to a large saucepan, along with the butter. Melt over a gentle heat. Add the sugar and vanilla, then add the eggs one at a time, mixing well after each addition. Add the flour and cocoa and mix until evenly combined.

Pour the mixture into a well-greased 24cm x 30cm baking tin. Bake 30–40 minutes until set.

Brownies are best cut while still slightly warm. I prefer to cut them into triangles – slice your slab into 4 strips lengthways, and 3 strips widthways, and then cut each square in half to make triangles.

Decorate with snow (sieved icing sugar).

. . . .

You can easily modify this basic brownie recipe by adding one of the following:

- 1 cup toasted nuts (page 40) – almonds, walnuts, hazelnuts or macadamias – roughly chopped

- white chocolate drops

- finely grated orange zest

Chocolate pots

Chocolate pots look adorable served in individual cups, glasses or dishes. I think they are best served in espresso or tea cups, but they can also be presented in polystyrene or plastic cups for easy cleanup. Conveniently, they can be made days before serving.

500g (18oz) chocolate, the best quality you can afford

3 oranges

50g (2oz) butter

4 tablespoons Grand Marnier or Cointreau (2 tablespoons for recipe and 2 tablespoons for decoration)

4 egg yolks & 2 egg whites

biscotti, optional

Zest one orange with a fine grater. Reserve one slice of another orange for decoration, then squeeze all three oranges until you have a half cup of juice.

Smash the chocolate while still in its wrapper. Put the broken chocolate, orange zest, juice and butter into the top of a double boiler (or a heat-resistant bowl placed over a pan of gently simmering water, making sure the water does not touch the bowl bottom).

Gently heat the mixture, stirring occasionally.

Remove from the heat and add 2 tablespoons of your chosen liqueur.

You can easily turn this jaffa-themed recipe into a mocha sensation. Simply replace the orange juice and zest with ½ cup cold espresso coffee (or plunger if you must), and use Kahlua, or any other coffee liqueur. Decorate with Kahlua and a few chocolate-covered coffee beans, or dollop with softly-whipped cream and sprinkle with cinnamon, cappuccino-style.

In a large bowl, beat together 4 egg yolks. Slowly add the cooled chocolate mixture, beating constantly. Allow the mixture to cool.

In a clean bowl, with a clean whisk, beat the 2 egg whites until stiff. Using a spatula, gently fold the whisked whites into the chocolate mixture. I find this easiest to do if I've added a dollop of the chocolate mixture to the egg whites first.

Pour the mixture into your chosen vessels. Cover and chill to set, about 2 hours.

Sprinkle a few drops of liqueur on each pot, and decorate with a wedge of the reserved slice of orange. Serve with your favourite biscotti if desired.

I remember my mother making these little pots of heaven on very special occasions. As we were not able to afford an entire bottle of Grand Marnier when I was young, my father would pop over to the local pub on a covert mission. He'd order a few nips of Grand Marnier, straight, and secret them away in a plastic container in his coat pocket. As I'm not endorsing such behaviour, I'll advise you that any brandy, cognac or even whisky from your liquor cabinet can be used as an alternative.

Drinks

There's often a temptation to serve glorious food but cut costs on drinks. Resist. When it comes to alcohol, you usually get what you pay for. It's better to serve a small quantity of a really terrific wine or cocktail than a large quantity of poor quality beverages. It's also wise to have a limited selection, so each style and flavour can be fully savoured and enjoyed.

The drinks list

Cocktails

Cocktails are obviously essential fare for formal cocktail parties, but they're also great to serve guests on arrival at any party. Champagne cocktails are especially good for this. There are many modern and classic cocktails, some of which are described in this chapter.

Bubbles

Whether French champagne or New Zealand méthode traditionelle or méthode champenoise, bubbles are far and away the most popular party drink, and the perfect way to greet guests. Make sure you keep some in reserve if you are having toasts or speeches. And bubbles must be cold.

White wine

White wine suits virtually all occasions and is the best choice to follow bubbles. A rule of thumb is: the bigger the food flavours, the stronger the wine characters that can be supported. Safe bets are sauvignon blanc and chardonnay. Varietals such as pinot gris, riesling and gewürztraminer are perfect for hot summer days. Serve white wine chilled.

Red wine

Red wine is usually not as popular at parties as other drinks, but demand increases in the winter. If you have pale carpet, you may not want to risk it. If red wine is spilled, generously coat the carpet with table salt and vacuum it away the next day. Pouring soda water on the stain has also been known to help, as has throwing a thick towel on top and jumping on it vigorously until the liquid is soaked up. Serve red wine at room temperature.

Beer

Beer is a must at parties where lads will be in attendance. Always serve bottled beer: cans and kegs are strictly for clubrooms. Choose beers you know are well liked by your guests. There is an enormous variety available from all over the world, as well as many interesting local brews. If you want a beer with style, try Mexican Corona, served with a wedge of lime or lemon in the neck of the bottle.

Non-alcoholic

Have plenty of iced water, mineral water and other non-alcoholic drinks. If you are providing orange juice, it is worthwhile getting freshly-squeezed. Be innovative – fruit nectar, ginger beer, lemon, lime and bitters and non-alcoholic punch, served in tall glasses with plenty of ice and interesting accompaniments such as lemon twists, can look and taste sensational.

Coffee

The smell of coffee brewing is a classic signal to guests that the party is wrapping up and it's time to think about heading home. Plunger coffee is the easiest to prepare and serve. Be sure to use freshly and specially ground coffee. Don't forget to have a selection of teas on hand as well.

Wine selection

As any caterer will tell you, it's impossible to predict how much people will drink. Even so, it's worth doing some planning – it will increase your confidence as a host. Here are some hints for making a beverage list:

A 750ml bottle of wine holds 5 good-size glasses.

White wine – have equal quantities of sauvignon blanc and chardonnay. In hot summer weather, consider one-third sauvignon blanc, one-third chardonnay, and one-third of a varietal such as gewürztraminer.

Red wine – a rule of thumb is one bottle of red wine for every three or four bottles of white.

Failsafe – you can't go wrong if you cater for three-quarters of a bottle, or even one bottle, of wine per person for a party which will last several hours, and have generous quantities of food. This may sound excessive but there's nothing worse than a dry bar when everything is going swimmingly. And don't worry if you over-purchase – many suppliers allow you to return unopened bottles. Arrange this when you purchase.

A rough guide might be:

10 guests	– 6 bottles of white wine, 2 bottles of red wine
20 guests	– 12 bottles of white wine, 4 bottles of red wine
50 guests	– 30 bottles of white wine, 10 bottles of red wine
100 guests	– 60 bottles of white wine, 20 bottles of red wine

Bring your own – if you are on a tight budget, don't be embarrassed to ask your guests to bring their own wine or beer, especially if you are providing all the food. You may like to provide a cocktail or glass of bubbles on arrival.

How to serve drinks

How you serve drinks will depend on whether your event is formal or informal:

full-service – pass drinks on trays, or set up a bar, using friends or staff to serve the drinks.

self-service – set up a designated place where guests can help themselves. Leave space for them to offload empty glasses and bottles.

To serve drinks you will need:

glasses – champagne flutes, wine glasses and tumblers. Hiring is a good option. For really casual affairs, it's acceptable to use plastic glasses.

jugs – for water, juice and other non-alcoholic drinks.

ice – a last-minute item you can pick up from your local service station.

garnishes – lemons and limes, mint leaves, berries and cherries, swizzle sticks and miniature umbrellas.

tools – bottle-openers, small knives, chopping boards, glass cloths and tea-towels.

trays – with non-slip surfaces or mats for formal drinks service. To hold a tray of drinks, carry the entire weight of the tray on your forearm, giving you enough control to hold the tray close to your body when moving through crowds.

cooling places – to keep bottles of beer or wine chilled without taking up valuable refrigerator space, store them in an ice-filled laundry sink, washing machine, bath, tub or buckets.

Classic champagne cocktail

This cocktail makes even the most economical bubbles taste like a luxurious elixir. Angostura Bitters (named after a port town in Venezuela) is a bittersweet blend of over forty herbs, plant extracts and spices. Bitters can be found in bottle stores, and you will recognise the small bottle by its strangely over-sized paper label. Use Bitters sparingly as it is strongly flavoured.

1 glass sparkling wine – méthode traditionelle, méthode champenoise or champagne

1 dash Angostura Bitters

2 tablespoons brandy

1 sugar cube

Place the sugar cube in a champagne flute. Add the brandy and dash of bitters. Carefully top with the sparkling wine.

You can vamp up any glass of sparkling wine by simply adding any of the following:

1 tablespoon Dubonnet Rouge, 2 dashes Angostura Bitters, 1 sugar cube (Dubonnet is a type of vermouth made in France from a mixture of wines, spices and herbs)

2 tablespoons syrup from any stewed or macerated fruits

1 tablespoon blended peaches, 1 tablespoon peach schnapps

1 tablespoon berry coulis, 1 tablespoon cassis

Retro fruit punch

Punch is an economical way to serve the masses, and avoids the fuss of individually made drinks. Tea, juice and fizzy form the base of this '60s-style punch. You can add as little or as much alcohol as desired.

up to 2 litres (8 cups) vodka, gin and/or white rum

1 litre (4 cups) cold tea

2 litres (8 cups) fruit juice – any combination of orange, apple, grapefruit

1.5 litres (6 cups) lemonade

1.5 litres (6 cups) ginger ale or ginger beer

250ml (1 cup) lime cordial or lemon cordial

1 handful mint leaves, torn

1 orange, sliced

2 lemons, sliced

4 handfuls ice cubes

If your refrigerator is anything like mine, full of booze and food, you won't be able to fit in all the juice and soft drink required for the punch. Keep the spirits in the freezer (they won't freeze) and add these and the ice at the last minute – both will cool the punch dramatically.

Mix all the liquid, mint and ice in a huge bowl. Decorate with the citrus slices and serve using a ladle.

Long Island iced tea

Long Island iced tea has a proven ability to cheer and enliven any partygoer. It gets its name from its infamous history. In American Prohibition days, heathens drank a blend of vodka and cola in tea cups in an effort to fool law enforcers. You can't but help feel a little devious consuming this brew. Beware, it is truly potent. You have been warned!

1 shot vodka

1 shot gin

1 shot white rum

1 shot white tequila

1 shot Triple Sec

juice of 1 lemon

lemon quarters for decoration

cola, to top up

ice cubes

In a cocktail shaker, combine the spirits, lemon juice and a few ice cubes. Shake, rattle and roll. Half fill a tall glass with ice cubes, strain the cocktail over the ice and top up with cola. Decorate with a lemon wedge and serve with a long straw.

A 1125ml spirit bottle holds around 30–40 shots (a shot is 1 ounce, 2 tablespoons or 30ml).

Feijoa-infused vodka with Ch'i

This is a thoroughly modern New Zealand cocktail, and wonderfully refreshing on a hot summer's evening. Feijoa-infused vodka can be easily made using the recipe below (or bought from liquor stores). Ch'i is a blend of New Zealand sparkling mineral water with Chinese herbs.

For the vodka

1125ml (4 generous cups) vodka, best quality

3 feijoas, quartered

Push the feijoa quarters into the vodka bottle, or combine the vodka and feijoa quarters in a jar. The feijoa-infused vodka will be ready for use after one week. Once ready it will last for ages.

To speed up the process, mash the feijoa and use after three days. In this scenario, the vodka has to be strained.

To serve

2 shots feijoa-infused vodka

Ch'i, to top up

ice

feijoa, kiwifruit or cucumber slices, to decorate

Half fill a tall glass with ice cubes, add 2 shots of feijoa-infused vodka and top up with Ch'i. Decorate with a slice of feijoa, kiwifruit or cucumber and serve with a long straw.

. . . .

You can easily infuse vodka with all sorts of other flavours:

berries – blackberries, raspberries, cranberries, strawberries, blueberries

fruit – kiwifruit, peaches and plums, passionfruit, cherries

spices – whole red chillies, vanilla beans, cinnamon quills, coffee beans

Drunken melon

I first saw this recipe being prepared and consumed on the television show *Beverly Hills 90210* when I was a teenager. I thought it was way cool, and couldn't wait to be old enough to try it. When I did, it lived up to my expectations – lots of fun to eat and deliciously intoxicating. Serve with plenty of large napkins to catch the drips.

750ml (3 cups) vodka or white rum, best quality

1 whole watermelon

Freeze any leftover drunken melon, seeds removed and cut into chunks. Blend with a few ice cubes to create a potent melon daiquiri, or serve as melon ice cube chasers.

Make a hole about the size of a two dollar coin in the rind of one side of the watermelon. Keep the piece of watermelon rind you have just cut out, to plug up the hole later.

Using a funnel, pour in as much vodka as the watermelon will take. Plug with the watermelon rind stopper.

Repeat the next hour, and the next hour, until no more vodka will fit. Use a piece of duct or gaffer tape to seal the plug.

Rotate the watermelon each hour to ensure even absorption.

Cut into slices to serve.

Margarita granita

Margarita granita is an adult slushy, perfect for fun in the sun. Triple Sec is a clear orange-flavoured liqueur. You can serve this 'dessert' at the beginning or end of a party.

3 cups water

1 cup sugar

4 limes, juice and finely grated zest

4 shots tequila, preferably gold

4 shots Triple Sec

½ cup pouring salt

3 limes, sliced, to serve

As a person who loves salt, I enjoy the salt on the rim of a margarita glass just as much as the contents. To make extra-special lime salt, place the 3 sliced limes with the ½ cup salt in a covered container. Let sit in a cool place for a week, mixing occasionally. Use the lime-flavoured salt for the glass rims, and the lime slices for decorating the glasses.

A 1125ml spirit bottle holds around 30–40 shots (a shot is 1 ounce, 2 tablespoons or 30ml).

Combine the water and sugar in a saucepan and make a syrup over a gentle heat. Allow to cool, then add the lime juice and zest, tequila and Triple Sec and stir.

Pour into a shallow dish – a very clean roasting dish or cake pan – and place in the freezer. Every 30 minutes aerate the granita using a fork, ensuring the more frozen parts get mixed into the unfrozen parts. The granita will take about 6 hours to become firm. Once it is firm, serve as soon as possible.

Prepare your glasses by salting the rims – dip them into a saucer of water then into a saucer of salt.

Scoop the margarita granita into the glasses. Decorate the glasses with lime slices – make a cut in each slice from the centre to the edge and slip this slit on to the edge of the glass.

Serve with teaspoons.

Index

Acknowledgements

Huge thanks to Lyndi, my food guru, and Ken, the human food disposal machine, for all your suggestions and support in the creation of this book. Words cannot express how much you mean to me, and how grateful I am to you for helping me become what I am today.

Thanks to Jane, Helen, Carly and Ray, the best friends a girl could have. Cooking with/for (delete as appropriate) you is always a pleasure.

Thanks to the Varnham O'Regan family – Mary, Paul, Chris, Sylvia and Ciaran – who have provided me with fantastic cooking challenges and opportunities. A special thanks to you Mary, for your vision of a fresh and friendly cookbook to help the everyday cook create great, fuss-free party food, and for all your hard work getting the show on the road.

I am greatly indebted to Anne Wendelken, 'grounded' food stylist, and Shaun Cato-Symonds, food photographer extraordinaire, for the very beautiful photographs.

I would also like to thank Celia Howden, who generously lent many of the props from her lovely Wellington store, Vessel, and Gill Gane of Neudorf Ceramics, who shipped her fine platters across Cook Strait.

Finally, I want to thank the many chefs and cooks whose shared experiences, books and television shows have stimulated and inspired my own cooking.